TOUGH
Questions
HONEST
Answers

TOUGH
Questions
HONEST
Answers

John C. Maxwell

Here's Life Publishers
P.O. Box 1576, San Bernardino, CA 92402

TOUGH QUESTIONS . . . HONEST ANSWERS
John Maxwell

Published by
HERE'S LIFE PUBLISHERS, INC.
P.O. Box 1576
San Bernardino, CA 92402

HLP Product No. 950964
© 1985, John Maxwell
All rights reserved.
Printed in the United States of America.

Library of Congress Cataloging-in-Publication Data

Maxwell, John (John C.)

Tough Questions — Honest Answers.
1. Wesleyan Church — Sermons.
2. Sermons, American.
    I. Title.
BX999.5W46M39   1985   252'.071   85-8677
ISBN 0-89840-085-6 (pbk.)

FOR MORE INFORMATION, WRITE:

L.I.F.E. — P.O. Box A399, Sydney South 2000, Australia
Campus Crusade for Christ of Canada — Box 300, Vancouver, B.C., V6C 2X3, Canada
Campus Crusade for Christ — 103 Friar Street, Reading RG1 1EP, Berkshire, England
Lay Institute for Evangelism — P.O. Box 8786, Auckland 3, New Zealand
Great Commission Movement of Nigeria — P.O. Box 500, Jos, Plateau State Nigeria, West Africa
Life Ministry — P.O. Box/Bus 91015, Auckland Park 2006, Republic of South Africa
Campus Crusade for Christ International — Arrowhead Springs, San Bernardino, CA 92414, U.S.A.

DEDICATION

This book is dedicated to the congregation at Skyline
Wesleyan Church, who
    open their Bibles with ready hearts
    listen to the Word with receptive ears and
    encourage their Pastor with radiant faces.

PREFACE

One pastor, speaking to another in an exasperated tone, said, "Just when I know all the answers my people start asking new questions!"

That's only too true for those of us who endeavor to minister weekly to people living in a rapidly changing world. It's not easy.

Charlie Brown found this out one day when Lucy came to him and said, "Life is a mystery, Charlie Brown. . .Do you know the answer?"

Charlie Brown answered, "Be kind. Don't smoke. Be prompt. Smile a lot. Eat sensibly. Avoid cavities and mark your ballot carefully. Avoid too much sun. Send overseas packages early. Love all creatures above and below. Insure your belongings and try to keep the ball low. . ."

Before he could get out another platitude, Lucy interrupted: "Hold real still," she said, "because I am going to hit you a very sharp blow upon your nose!"

Lucy didn't want pat answers to her complex question. Her deep needs requested deep thought and a careful response. She is like many Christians today.

My desire as senior pastor of Skyline Wesleyan Church is to endeavor to answer some of the difficult questions that my congregation is asking. Many times while preaching I ask myself, "Am I meeting their deep-seated needs?" After wrestling with this question for several months I came up with the following solution.

Each spring I ask the congregation to write down the subject they would like me to cover from the pulpit. My assistant, Barbara Brumagin, lists all the subjects, and the top ten requests form my summer preaching schedule.

The response has been amazing! Our summer attendance grows instead of showing the usual vacation "fall out." Members have even rearranged vacations so they could hear "their subjects."

I believe that many of the chapters in this book will also be "your subject." The best writing comes from experiences that the author has lived. These chapters deal with questions I too have asked myself. The best reading comes from a personal interest that the reader senses in his life. No doubt some of these chapters were written just for you.

John Maxwell

CONTENTS

CHAPTER 1

How Can
I Cope With
Pressure And Stress?

Stress is a reality in our life. Can you think of at least one stressful situation you had to deal with during this last week? Perhaps you would rather not think about it.

In his book, *Self Help,* David Stoop has an entire section on stress and what it can do to us. He says that 40 million allergies a year are stress related. Thirty million people suffer from hypertension; 20 million have ulcers; and one out of three Americans suffer from being overweight because of stress. Two hundred thirty million prescriptions for tranquilizers are filled each year. One person in ten has a serious alcohol problem which in some way is related to stress. According to medical research, 75-90 percent of all illnesses are caused by stress in modern life.

One of the beautiful things about the Word of God is that it doesn't leave us hanging. The world can quote the statistics, but after they have been quoted, basically it's up to us to do the best we can to cope. What is beautiful about God's word is that we can take it and apply it to our lives and receive help.

No one is immune to negative stress. Christians are human and, as such, they are vulnerable to human foibles and problems. Problems cause stress.

Researchers have catalogued more than 100 major causes of stress. These causes fall primarily into three basic categories: (1) *life changes* (marriage, divorce, separation, death of a loved one, sickness or personal injury); (2) *work-related factors* (promotions, transfers, job loss, new responsibilities); and (3) *environmental problems* (pollution, crime, noise, weather, living conditions).

The secret to handling stress is to understand yourself and to be able to know when you're getting near the "danger threshold." That's the point where stress becomes harmful, and when normal stress develops into distress. There are several signs or signals that appear when you get close to this area of harm.

When you get under harmful stress, your body will not assimilate new information it is given. You stop listening as you should. You don't remember things you should. In effect, you become overloaded and begin to burn out mentally and emotionally.

Similarly, your mental horizons begin to close in. Although God has given you a creative mind that serves as a problem solver, instead of seeing potential solutions to the problems, you start to see problems in every solution. Your creativity reaches a dead end. You no longer see alternative courses to action. You feel stalemated in the battle against life's negative factors.

Often you will begin to think back to better days and times. Sometimes a person can even become childish — breaking things, pouting. In adult life, these responses can be self-destructive. Some people lose the ability to rid themselves of these harmful habits. They cannot make positive changes. For example, when under heavy stress we all have a hard time saying no. Therefore, we often wind up increasing our work load instead of decreasing it. Ironically, we seem to think this will help us work ourselves out of the pressure cooker.

We become weary. We wake up in the morning still tired. When we are under excessive stress, our body craves more rest than usual. We toss and turn at night. The fatigue we feel compounds itself. Ultimately, we experience fits of depression and grief and great bouts of anxiety. Unless reversed, these symptoms eventually can lead to nervous breakdowns, phobias, or feelings of complete alienation from the world.

Some researchers believe that 70 percent of all physical illness is related to stress. In progressing through the danger signals of stress, we get into the area we referred to earlier as burnout. There are five signs or signals that indicate a developing phase of burnout in your life.

1. *Decreased energy.* You know what should be done but you just don't have the energy or the pizzazz to do it.

2. *Feelings of failure.* You begin to feel overwhelmed with feelings of failure and of not being able to measure up. You feel you aren't accomplishing what you should. You begin to judge yourself harshly.

3. *Reduced sense of reward.* Even when you are rewarded for something you have done well, you don't feel as though the reward is adequate. Your sense of competition disappears. You aren't motivated to be the top dog at anything anymore.

4. *Sense of helplessness.* You begin to feel there is no way out. You carry with you a constant sense of helplessness, of being out of control.

5. *Cynicism and negativism.* You have a tendency to become cynical and bitter, to look at life with a negative view. You focus on only the bad part of life.

These are the traits of a person going through the burnout stage caused by stress. What does God's word say that can help the Christian handle stress? In Philippians 4:6,7, Paul tells us not to worry about anything, but, instead, to pray about everything. He talks about our anxieties and worries. Philippians is a good book to read if you're having stress problems. I think the apostle Paul provides the best pattern to follow if you want to find somebody who knew how to handle stress. I have found his letters offer the best advice on handling pressure.

Paul reminds us, "Trust in the Lord. . . .Rejoice always. . . . He is able to do exceedingly abundantly. . . .My God shall supply all of your need. . . . I can do all things through Christ who strengthens me." There are many great and positive phrases in the writings of Paul. Then you can go over to the Gospels and listen to the words of Jesus and they also have a comforting effect.

Jesus says, "Seek ye first the kingdom of God, and His righteousness, and all these things shall be added unto you" (Matt. 6:33, KJV). He talks about seeing the sparrow when it falls and counting the hairs on your head. He sees the lily in the fields. He tells us to take no thought of tomorrow — tomorrow will take care of itself. Don't be anxious. He says, "Ask, seek and knock, and it will be opened unto you."

When we read the writings of Paul and hear the words of Jesus, they offer a familiar ring to us as Christians. The fact that there is a biblical answer to stress helps us endure.

Not all tension and not all stress is harmful. There is an amount of tension that is good for us. In fact, I am the type of person who does better under pressure than without it. My life is truly not very comfortable if I don't have a certain amount of pressure to motivate me. I seem to function better under pressure. It can be a very creative thing and it helps me be more productive. Perhaps you are the same way.

I enjoy going to hear the San Diego Pops Orchestra at Mission Bay in the summer. At first, when the musicians are getting their instruments ready to play, they tighten the violin strings. The process sounds terrible. But when they have the right tension (not too much, not too little) those strings begin to produce beautiful music. That's the way it is in our lives, too. We need just the right amount of tension to make things harmonize.

In Psalm 37 the first three words have always grabbed me: "Do not fret." That word "fret" means to eat away or to gnaw away or to wear away. Negative stress always will erode our lives.

The best way to define negative anxiety and stress is to use a car as an example. Suppose you go out and turn on the engine of your car. Instead of putting the gear into drive, you keep it in park or neutral. You trounce the accelerator to the floor, release it, trounce it, release it, trounce it. The engine roars and fades. It races, grows hot, overheats and begins to smoke. You generate a lot of noise and smog but you get nowhere. In fact, you accomplish nothing more than ruining a perfectly good engine.

The human body works in a similar way. If you rev up your heart and nerves and brain waves with constant worry, stress and anxiety, you'll go nowhere (and you'll ruin a perfectly good body).

I remember that as a kid I must have put 2,000 miles on my dad's car going back and forth in the driveway. It was fun for me, but it caused strain on both the car and my father's wallet.

Charlie Brown can be quite a theologian at times. Linus was dragging his blanket one day and said, "Charlie Brown, you look kind of depressed."

Charlie Brown replied, "I worry about school a lot." He paused. "I worry about my worrying about school. Even my anxieties have anxieties."

Instead of sitting and musing over my anxieties, I have found another human way of handling stress. Let me share it with you.

Before I left my last church, where my associate, Aaron, was to take the senior pastorate position, I trained him for several months. One day I sat him down and asked if there was anything more I could share with him. He said, "There is one thing I need to know. I have worked side by side with you and I never have seen you get upset. I never see you crack under pressure. When everyone else is hitting his head against the wall, I never see you uptight and frustrated. You just walk around and smile as if nothing is wrong. How do you handle this pressure?"

I told him to follow me. I led him through a maze of offices, back to where my private office was. Once in the office, I locked the door behind us. I laid down on the nice carpet. Aaron couldn't believe what he was seeing. I said, "When I really get under pressure and stress, I do this." I began to flail my arms and kick my feet and yell, "aaa-hhh-a-a-a-hhhh!"

I then got up, buttoned my coat, smiled, unlocked the door, and walked through the office smiling and greeting the secretaries. Aaron followed me, chuckling and shaking his head.

Last month I met with him and asked him how it was going. He said the church was doing wonderfully and that he was pleased. He said, "John, the one trick you showed me that has helped me most. . . ."

We both broke out laughing. I said, "You don't mean you. . .?"

He nodded. "Almost every day."

Now, maybe you're not able to do that. Or maybe you don't want to do that. Fine. There are plenty of other options. Psalm 37 tells of some things you can do that will help you. Here are some of those suggestions:

Commit Your Way Unto the Lord

When the psalmist says "commit," he is speaking of revealing. Often we want to take this passage of Scripture and twist it a little bit and say that "commit" means to give. It doesn't here. It means to reveal. He is saying something like this, "Reveal to God your problems and your tensions." He's asking for an openness, a transparency, an honesty. He says, "Reveal your weaknesses. Come out with it."

Now, that's not easy for us to do. The natural tendency when we are under pressure is to hide it. We are taught to grin and bear it. Boys and men especially are taught to be tough — endure, survive, never cry.

Because of this, we take the stress we're under and cover it over, put a false smile on our face, throw back our shoulders and act macho. We laugh at the idea that we may need some help.

Us? Weak? Never! That's the natural tendency. Cover it and carry it. The world says, when you're under pressure and tension, bear it (or drug it). But God says, deal with it.

Sometimes the world will suggest that you "find yourself." Go under therapy and counseling. Now, therapy certainly has a valid place in the life of a Christian. But God's word goes a little bit further. Not only should we review our problems but we should also reveal it. Get it out. Don't just continually fuss; do something with it. The world would say carry it, carry those pressures. But the Word of God says commit it. Develop a revealing heart toward God and lay out to Him what your pressures really are. He does care. Oswald Chambers has said, "All our fret and worry is caused by calculating without God."

Trust In Him and He Will Do It

Let's look at this word "trust." If commit means to reveal, trust means to release. The indication of trust is the willingness to give something that you hold very special to someone else. When you have a friend with whom you have a trusted relationship, basically what you have is a friend you believe in so much that you can trust him with anything. This is where the commitment comes in, where giving comes in. I can paraphrase that last part of verse 5 to read, "God will accomplish all that you release to Him." In other words, if you don't release it, He can't relieve it. Our problem is not a God who cannot relieve our tensions and pressures. Our problem is being a people unable to release ourselves to Him.

Our tendency is to give in to Him at a moment of extreme frustration and helplessness, only to pick everything up again when we are "feeling better," or are "getting on top of things." We think we've got everything under control. Isn't that a joke? I've never had a day in my life in which I've had everything under control! Doesn't God have a fabulous sense of humor?

Whenever I think I've got it all under control, God brings one more dimension into my life. The moment we think we're strong, doesn't He have the ability to show us we're really weak? The moment we think we've got all the answers, doesn't He have some of the best questions?

For me to trust is for me to get to the point where I learn to release. This is a personal release, not me releasing your problems to God. That's easy. You come with your set of problems and pressures and what do I say? "Well," I say, "give them to God!" And I can sound very pious as I do so. Sure, I can say that. Why not? The problems aren't mine. I'm like the general who told his troops, "I'm behind you all the way, men," and then whispered to his aide, "Make sure that I'm *way* behind them."

This trusting isn't my taking your pressures and giving them to God. It's each of us dealing with our own pressures. This isn't pastoral; this is personal. Too many times we're like the man who prayed, "Lord, I will give you my family." Nothing happened. More desperately he prayed, "Lord, I will give you my business." Nothing happened. Finally in total desperation he said. "Lord, I will give you myself." Then something happened! Turn things over to Him. He said commit, which means "to reveal" your pressures. He said trust, which means "to release" them. And He said more:

Delight Yourself in the Lord; and He Will Give You the Desires of Your Heart

Commit means to reveal; trust means release; delight means rejoice. Rejoice? Get happy. You say, "Wait a minute. Now you've gone off the deep end, preacher. The subject is pressure, stress and problems. And now you're trying to tell us to get happy?"

Do me a favor. Underline two words in that verse in your Bible; "delight" and "desires." It's very important to know those two words. It's important to understand their order, too. The sequences of these two words makes all the difference between a religion of selfishness and a religion of love.

Watch this: This verse does not say, "The Lord will give you what your heart desires; therefore, delight in Him." It does not say, "Tell the Lord what you want and He'll give it to you." This verse does not try to portray God as a theological Santa Claus.

Delight is an act of the *will*. Emotions are only the result of your choosing to "delight." The psalmist said that if you want to start delighting in God, you should put your delight where it *should* be; if you put your love and affection on that level, *then* God will begin to do a work in your life, and regardless of where you are, you will be able to rejoice! That's why Paul is able to say in Romans 8:38, "I have become absolutely convinced that neither death nor life, neither messenger of heaven, nor monarch of earth, neither what happens today nor what may happen tomorrow, neither a power from on high nor a power from below, nor anything else in God's whole world has any power to separate us from the love of God in Christ Jesus our Lord" (Phillips).

You see, Paul demonstrated that it is our commitment, not our circumstance that gives us joy. I'm telling you, I know some of the happiest people who have bad situations. And I know some of the unhappiest people who are in absolutely super situations. We're always saying, "If I only had. . ." or "If we could only get. . ." or "If I could just be given. . . ." We yearn for what others have rather than rejoice in our own blessings.

Paul wrote a special letter to the church at Philippi. "Rejoice in the Lord!" he told the Philippians. And where was he writing from? Not from the Hotel del Coronado. From prison! A guy who was in chains in the dungeon was writing to people who were walking around in the sunlight without chains, "Hey, get happy out there!" Isn't it amazing?

I run into people all the time who say, "If I could just have this in life I could get happy." But if you are unhappy where you are, you'll be unhappy anywhere. If you're unhappy married, you're going to be unhappy single. If you're not happy single, you're going to be unhappy married. And if you're unhappy when you're poor, you're going to be unhappy when you are rich. And if you're unhappy rich, you'll *certainly* be unhappy poor.

The psalmist in Psalm 37 is trying to teach us something about stress. He is saying it isn't your *problem* that brings you stress. It's your perspective of that problem. It's how you look at your problems. Let me illustrate that. When I was growing up my brother and I had to do the dishes at the house. We had a sister who was seven years younger and we could hardly wait until she "became of age." There were times that I would do the dishes with my brother and because he was older and bigger he would get his choice as to whether he would wash or dry. I'd grumble while I worked whatever was designated to me. I hated to do dishes.

I was dating Margaret at that time. There were times when I would hurry to do the dishes after the dinner hour so I could get in the car and go twenty miles to Chillicothe to see the girl I loved. I'd run into the house and there would be Margaret. . . doing dishes. Hey, no problem. I would get in there and grab that dishtowel and I would dry those dishes and we'd have a good time talking about how things were that week. I'd reach over and give her a peck on the cheek and just keep on doing those dishes. We had the best time. Wash, dry, put away. . .whooppee. What made the difference? Not the dishes! The difference was the delight. The scenery was beautiful. The rewards were great.

That's exactly what God is trying to teach us through Psalm 37 when He tells us, "I'll show you how to handle stress." Just fall head over heels in love with God until your opening thought in the morning is, "THIS IS THE DAY THAT THE LORD HATH MADE! I WILL REJOICE AND BE GLAD IN IT!" As you go through the routine, mundane things, and average activities of life, there will be a spark — not because you have a good day or a bad day or because it was Monday or Sunday, but because all day your affection and heart have been set upon the God who is above all else, the God who loves and cares for you. That's the difference! Delight in Him.

Rest in the Lord

Commit means reveal; trust means release; delight means rejoice; rest means readiness. I'm not talking about a rest from action. I'm talking about a rest from friction. There's a lot of difference between resting for the Lord and rusting in the Lord.

The philosopher Kierkegaard told the story of a handsome drake who grew bored flying south with the other ducks each fall. So, on one trip, he landed in a barnyard and joined a group of mixed fowl and spent the winter sharing their cornfeeder and haylofts. When spring came and the wild ducks flew northward again, the handsome drake tried to rejoin his friends. His wings were weak and his stomach was fat. He could fly no higher than the barn roof. By opting for earthbound security, he'd forfeited his ability to soar.

Christians sometimes are like the unwise duck. They misunderstand the real meaning of resting in the Lord. It does not mean being content and lazy. Instead, it means having confidence in God's strength and being ready to respond to His every call.

Dwell in the Land and Cultivate Faithfulness

Commit means reveal; trust means release; delight means rejoice; rest means readiness; dwell means remain.

Remain. Stay right there. The psalmist had said commit, reveal, trust, delight, rest, or get into a state of readiness for what God wants you to do in the process of the pressure, but also dwell. Stay right where you are. The human tendency when we're under pressure is to panic, to run. Removal is the first thing that comes to mind, but God says, "Remain." I used to look at verse 3 and read, "Dwell in the land and develop faithfulness" and be naive and think that "faithfulness" was already mine. But we need to stay where we are in order for faithfulness to develop. Stick it out. That's what it means.

Here's my paraphrase, "Remain where you are and see the faithfulness of God." We cultivate the faithfulness of God in our lives. In short, "Don't just do something: stand there." Let God do His work. God is going to get a lot more blessing from Daniel while he is in the lions' den than when he is removed from it. God is going to get a greater blessing out of the Hebrew children in the fire than after they are removed from it.

The great thing about Christian living is found in Psalm 66. In verse 12, there is a truth about stress and pressure: "We went *through* fire, and *through* water; yet Thou didst bring us out into a place of *abundance.*" The difference between a Christian and a non-Christian in this area of stress is this: The non-Christian doesn't go *through* the water, he drowns in it! The non-Christian is consumed by the fire, but the Christian goes through it.

"Through it all, through it all, I've learned to trust in Jesus, I've learned to trust in God."* Have you learned that in the area of stress? There's a song we used to sing as kids. It's called *God Leads His Dear Children Along.* It says, "Some through the waters, some through the flood, some through the fire, but all through the blood; some through great sorrow, but God gives a song, in the night season and all the day long."

With the song God gives, we all can handle the day-to-day stresses of life.

CHAPTER 2

Can
We Receive
Guidance From God Today?

Psalm 143 helps us to know God's will for our lives. It is important for Christians to consider how to know His will, how to discern His will, how to walk in His will. Why? Because it is in the center of God's will that we find true growth and Christian contentment and effectiveness.

In Psalm 143, beginning at verse 8, the psalmist in his prayer for help says, "Let me hear Thy lovingkindness in the morning; for I trust in Thee; teach me the way in which I should walk; for to Thee I lift up my soul. Deliver me, O Lord, from my enemies; I take refuge in Thee. Teach me to do Thy will, for Thou art my God; let Thy good Spirit lead me on level ground." The three phrases we need to look at as we ask the question, "Can we receive guidance from God today?" are as follows:

Verse 8: "Let me hear"
Verse 8: "Teach me the way"
Verse 10: "Teach me to do"

Whenever you read one of David's psalms you immediately sense that he has been with God. You cannot read a psalm without beginning to feel that you are reading the words of a man who has spent time alone with the Lord. That's one of the main characteristics of David's writings. You find in verse 1 that David

23

spent time in prayer; "Hear my prayer, O Lord." In verse 5 we
see that he spent time in meditation: "I remember the days of old;
I meditate on all Thy doings; I muse on the work of Thy hands."

In verse 6 we see that David has spent time expressing his
love: "I stretch out my hands to Thee; my soul longs for Thee,
as a parched land." Beginning in verse 7 we see David has spent
time in communication and tells God he needs an answer quickly,
"Do not hide Thy face from me. . .let me hear. . .teach me the
way. . .teach me to do Thy will." It's very easily understood when
you look at this Scripture that there is a correlation between
relationship and communication. As we spend time with God we
begin to understand the will of God for our lives.

David provides several acknowledgments in this passage that
make his walk with God and this known will of God a reality in
his life. In verse 1 we can see that David acknowledges God's
faithfulness and His righteousness. In fact, he says in the last part
of verse 1, "Answer me with Thy faithfulness, in Thy righteousness."
What a way to be answered. In verse 2 he recognizes his own
unrighteousness: "For in Thy sight no man living is righteous."
In verse 3 he understands Satan's power: "For the enemy has
persecuted my soul; he has crushed my life to the ground; he has
made me dwell in dark places, like those who have long been
dead." In verse 4, because of the power of the enemy, he expresses
his weariness, his oppression, "Therefore my spirit is overwhelmed
within me; my heart is appalled within me."

About the time he is going to give up he realizes what God
has done for him in the past. "I remember the days of old; I
meditate on all Thy doings; I muse on the work of Thy hands."
Because of God's workings in days past, in verse 6, he expresses
his longing for God, "My soul longs for Thee." In verse 7, he
expresses his lostness without God's revealed will for his life:
"Answer me quickly, O Lord, my spirit fails; do not hide Thy
face from me, lest I become like those who go down to the pit."
In this passage David gives us three phrases that I want us to
notice. They will help us to understand that even in our day God
still does guide us.

TEACH ME TO HEAR — Level 1: Listening

"Let me hear Thy lovingkindness in the morning." David is
listening to the voice of God concerning His will for David's life.

Isn't it interesting that in verse 1 David was afraid God would not hear him? In verse 8 David is afraid he will not hear God. In eight verses we see that God has begun to change the heart of David.

I can apply that to my own prayer life. When I sense the need to go to prayer, it is not to listen to God. Too often my need to go to prayer is not to hear God; it's to bring my requests to Him. I can hardly wait to get alone with God and begin to list all the things I want God to do in my life. So for twenty-eight minutes I'll give him that huge list and say, "Hear this one, God. Listen to his one. Take care of this need. Listen to this request."In the winding down time, I usually reserve a couple of minutes to maybe quietly listen to what He is going to say. This is tragic because when we talk to God we only say something we already know. When we listen, we learn what God knows. I want us to understand that in trying to know the will of God we will need to spend a lot of time just listening to the voice of God, just being silent and knowing who He is.

In distinguishing the difference between listening and hearing, a high school student said, "Listening is wanting to hear." That is what David was doing. He wanted to hear the voice of God as He spoke to him. This may seem a little elementary, but Jesus was once talking to a group of people and as He shared with them He realized that they did not want to hear what He was saying. Jesus said, "He that has ears, let him hear." When I was a kid my mind used to go wild with that verse. I could see Jesus talking to a bunch of earless people. In my imagination, ladies wore earrings from their chins. Well, obviously, everybody in the crowd had ears. That isn't what Jesus was saying. He meant that it does no good to reveal God's will to you if you are not going to respond to that will.

You see, God's revelation must have a response. Or as the old proverb says, "You can lead a horse to water but you can't make him drink." You and I will never begin to know the will of God until we have a heart that is receptive to the voice of God.

There are several hindrances to this listening:

Traditions. When we have always done something in a specific way, it is difficult for us to listen to the freshness of His voice. We should try, though.

We don't want to know His will. We're not ready for the message of His will. There are times He shares His will and it is exactly contrary to what we want to hear.

Our impatience or restlessness. That's why the psalmist says to "cease striving and know that I am God." That's why Isaiah said that we are to be still, to wait upon Him. As we wait upon Him, He will renew our strength. In other words, as we noted in chapter one there are times in our prayer lives when we shouldn't just do something. We should stand there and wait on Him.

A lack of interest. It is possible that we aren't interested in knowing what He is saying, so we are not on "the same wavelength." One pastor was trying to explain the difference between fact and faith. "That you are sitting before me in the pew is *fact.* That I am speaking from the pulpit is *fact.* But it is only *faith* that makes me believe that anyone is listening." The psalmist knew that to know the will of God he must get on level 1, the level of listening.

TEACH ME TO KNOW — Level 2: Learning

We see in the middle part of verse 8, "Teach me the way in which I should walk." Now David has left the listening stage and is coming to the learning stage. He wants to learn what God's will is for his life. My own translation of Romans 12:2 is, "Do not conform to this present age but be transformed by the entire renewal of your mind so that you may learn by experience what God's will is for your life." We are to be learning the will of God, and that never ceases. As we walk with God, we learn the will of God. It is not possible to learn it all in one sitting. Learning the will of God requires walking with God, always learning, always listening. We learn through exploration (discovering new truths through experience). We learn through trial and error. We learn from the example of others.

Now there are several reasons why we need to learn and know about the will of God for our lives.

1. *The will of God is the only place for effective ministry.* The only time you and I become effective in our Christian ministry is when we're in the will of God. These three circles represent what I am talking about.

GOD'S WILL

Salvation

God's Ministry Will

God's Specific Ministry Will

The closer to the middle, the more we are effective and protected.

The outside circle is God's will. That's salvation. He is not willing that any should perish. It is God's will for each one of us to be saved. Then God has a ministry will for each of us. That's the next circle. We're getting a little closer to being "on target" when we not only know God's will for our lives but God's ministry will, too. For example, God's ministry will for me is to be a pastor.

Finally, there is God's specific ministry will and that is the smallest of all the circles. That is not only knowing what your gifts are and how to use them, but it is also finding a place to use them. That is, for myself, not only being in the pastoral ministry, but in the place where I should be to do that pastoral work. If your gift is teaching, it is not only that you have discovered your gift, but that you also are using that gift in the right class or right place. You should be in His perfect, specific ministry for your life. The closer you come to that last inner circle, the more productive you will become, the happier you will be, and the more impact you will have. Your life is most effective when you know you are right where God wants you.

2. *The will of God is the only place of fellowship.* D. L. Moody's life is a constant inspiration to me. One day Moody heard a knock on his study door. "Come in," he said. His young son entered. "Yes, son, what is it you want?"

"I don't want anything," came the answer, "but just to be with you."

Oh, how many Christians there seem to be whose comings to God in prayer are little more than repeated applications to *get* something from Him! Their self-impoverished souls know nothing about that "just to *be with you*" longing of Moody's little son, or about the deep, utter joy of just being *with* God is in secret fellowship.

A father and his young son were on a journey and were staying overnight somewhere far from home. They occupied separate beds in the same room. "Son, you seem restless. Is anything troubling you?"

The boy answered by asking, "Father, is your face turned toward me?"

"Yes, son, it is."

Without another sound the boy fell asleep. Nothing satisfies the true child of God like the loving look of the Father's face; and even if for that alone, being in the will of God means everything. It is His will for us to relate to Him and have fellowship together. So, therefore, He wants to reveal His will to us so we can have fellowship, that communion that is so necessary.

3. *Being within the will of God is the best place to be.* We need to learn God's will because it is the only place of assurance for our lives. One of the reasons we need to know we are in the center of His will is that when problems occur, it is the only thing that holds firm. You will be more effective in handling the problems you encounter in your Christian ministry and life if you know you are where God wants you to be.

4. *The will of God is the only place of self-fulfillment.* Since God alone knows us through and through — all our strengths and frailties — no one else can guide and develop us as He can. He alone knows just what kind of place and service will effect for us a maximum return on our invested talents. To have our *own* will and way often seems much freer and more grand, but that is because we cannot see as far as God does. The most spacious of all true self-realization is inside our heavenly Father's plan for us. It gives to all we do the touch of immortality. Inside that will, nothing we do ever dies, for God is in it. Yes, that is the place of utmost self-fulfillment and, therefore, of fullest satisfaction.

5. *The will of God is the only place where we can effectively build God's kingdom.* God has a special place for each of us. When you understand how the body of the Lord Jesus Christ works, that we are dependent upon each other, and that your gifts can complement the Church, your joy of Christian ministry will begin. In America we make a hero out of a man who is independent. We like that self-made man and we put him on a pedestal. But for a Christian, there is no such thing as a self-made man. There

is no such thing as a church that grows by itself, or a church that grows because of one person. It grows because many people are working together, loving each part of the body of Christ, each finding a place to serve.

Do you remember in 1969 when they finally put a man on the moon? I'll never forget it. When they panned the cameras around the Houston control center and we could see engineers and scientists and mathematicians, men of great minds, jumping up and down, throwing their coats around, hugging each other. They were hugging and loving because all of a sudden they understood that together they had accomplished what they could not have done alone.

The greatest thing that can happen to you is to find God's will for your life, find your gift, and then become part of the body of the Lord Jesus Christ. You can't be the whole thing. But because you, like others, share your gift, you can help do something that can be accomplished only as a team. Do you recall when Edmund Hillary and his native guide, Tenzing, made their historic climb up Mt. Everest? Coming down from the peak Hillary suddenly lost his footing. Tenzing held the line taut and kept them both from falling by digging his ax into the ice. Later Tenzing refused any special credit for saving Hillary's life; he considered it a routine part of the job. As he put it: "Mountain climbers always help each other." Should the rest of us be any different?

"There isn't a single person in the world who can make a pencil," insists Newsweek columnist Milton Friedman as he opens his new television series, "Free to Choose." The wood may have come from a forest in Washington, the graphite from a mine in South America, the eraser from a Malaysian rubber plantation. "Thousands of people cooperate to make one pencil."

What's causing so much disharmony in the church world is the fact that some want to beat the big drum, few are willing to face the music, and none will play second fiddle. Our goal as Christians, however, is to find God's will for our lives and just to lift one another up and love one another rather than to seek any special honor for ourselves.

TEACH ME TO DO — Level 3: Loving

Look at Psalm 143:10, "Teach me to *do* your will." You may be saying, "You mean to tell me that doing and loving are the same thing?" Absolutely. That's exactly what I mean.

Jesus understood that when He looked at Peter (in John 21) and said, "Do you love me?"

Peter answered, "Oh, you know I do."

But before Peter could slip into religious sentimentalism, Jesus said, "Peter, if you love Me, you'll feed my sheep." In other words Jesus challenged Peter to back up his claims of love with some action.

In Matthew chapter 7, Jesus talks about the fact that if we know God's will, we are to do God's will. He is teaching us that it is our action, our loving Him, or (as James says) our works, that show and demonstrate our faith. In Matthew 7:20 we read, "You will know them by their fruits. Not everyone who says to me 'Lord, Lord,' will enter the kingdom of heaven; but he who does the will of My Father who is in heaven." Then in verse 22 He tells us that paying lip service to Christianity is easy. "Many will say to Me on that day, 'Lord, Lord, did we not prophecy in Your name, and in Your name cast out demons, and in Your name perform many miracles?' And I will declare to them, 'I never knew you; depart from Me you who practice lawlessness.'"

Look at verse 24, "Therefore everyone who hears these words of mine and acts upon them, may be compared to a wise man, who built his house upon the rock. And the rain descended, and the floods came, and the winds blew and burst against that house; and yet it did not fall, for it had been founded upon the rock."

You see, the way to be strong, to be founded upon a good and firm foundation, is not only to hear the Word of God, but also as He reveals His will to you, to become active in Christian service. That's where you'll grow.

In Psalm 143 David said, "Teach me to hear." He said, "God, I'm listening."

In Psalm 143:8 he said, "Teach me to know." He said, "God, I'm learning."

In Psalm 143:10 he said, "Teach me to do." He said, "God, I'm loving."

CHAPTER 3

How Can
I Get Out of
My Holding Pattern **?**

The only sort of holding I enjoy is holding my wife Margaret and my two children. Otherwise, I don't want to be involved in holding up anything or have anything hold me up. I'm busy, aggressive and time-conscious.

If I call somewhere and the operator asks me if I would mind being put on hold, even fifteen seconds can seem an eternity to me. I'll never forget the time I was away at a conference and I called back home to my church; the new secretary didn't recognize my voice, and I wound up being put on hold by my own office.

In truth, I'm really not an impatient person, just someone who understands the value of time. But even I can overdo my conscientiousness now and then. For example, a few years ago I was on an airplane to Chicago which was put into a holding pattern above O'Hare Airport. It was vitally important for me to made a connecting flight to New York City. As we continued to circle over Chicago for fifteen minutes, thirty minutes, forty-five minutes, then an hour, I grew more and more upset and anxiety-ridden. Each time the stewardess would pass, I'd ask, "How much longer will this go on? When will we be landing? Will my connection hold for me?" Eventually, I must have worn away the dear girl's reserve of patience. She finally looked coldly at me and said, "As far as I'm concerned, mister, you can get out right now." All of a sudden, the holding pattern didn't seem so bad.

There is something frustrating and exasperating about the holding patterns we encounter in life. We need to learn how to break out of them. David Livingstone is one of my spiritual heroes. He, of course, was the missionary doctor whom God used so greatly in Africa. Livingstone said one time, "I will go anywhere, as long as it's forward."

Oliver Wendell Holmes once noted, "The great thing in this world is not so much where we stand, but what direction we are moving." Ralph Waldo Emerson wrote, "Man's life is a progress, not a station." I can identify with these kinds of men. They break out of holding patterns, crash through barriers, leap over obstacles. They believe in advancing at all times.

Charlie Brown and Lucy Van Pelt were on a cruise one day. As they stood on the ship's deck, Lucy thought she should use this opportunity to expound on the nature of human beings. She said, "Charlie Brown, look at the front part of this ship. The people in the bow are unfolding their deck chairs; these are the kinds of people who think of the future; they want to move forward; they are progressive. Now look at the people at the stern of the ship. They're looking backward. They are the people who are traditional; they like to look at the past and to review where they've been."

Lucy then asked the penetrating question, "Charlie Brown, where are you going to put *your* deck chair?" Charlie Brown, in frustrated simplicity, responded, "I don't know. I can't even get mine unfolded."

As Christians, many of us can identify with poor Charlie Brown. Before we can break out of our holding patterns and head in some direction, we need to overcome the simple obstacles in life that got us into the holding pattern to begin with. First things first, eh?

There are two kinds of spiritual holding patterns. There is the legitimate one that keeps us at a certain level until we are fully prepared to move on to a greater challenge; and there is the illegitimate one that makes us decide to do limited service to God.

In Isaiah 40:31 we read, "Those who wait for the Lord will gain new strength; they will mount up with wings like eagles, they will run and not get tired, they will walk and not become weary." There is the legitimate holding pattern — the one that helps us and honors God. We like it because we realize it is spiritually profitable for us.

LEGITIMATE HOLDING PATTERNS

There are several reasons why God occasionally opts to put us into a legitimate holding pattern:

For Preparation

To be better prepared to do the work in the ministry God has for us, there is a holding pattern we must be in which gives us time to develop our talents, wisdom, and experience. Moses serves as an example for us of a person in this kind of holding pattern. He spent forty years serving God in the wilderness. Similarly, Paul wandered in the Arabian desert praying, witnessing and studying. Jesus Himself retreated to the garden for communion with God and to the desert to be tempted and thus to gain strength to do battle against Satan.

There are times when God will put us into the holding pattern of life — three years of military service, four years as a Sunday school superintendent, two weeks as a vacation Bible school teacher, nine years as a shop foreman, two years as a city politician — so that we will gain the experience and depth of knowledge needed for whatever the next challenge is that He has in store for us. We must recognize these holding patterns as learning periods and redeem the time by learning all we possibly can. They are meant to be times of growth, not routine procedures.

For Mercy and Grace

All the time that Noah was building the ark, God's message was being preached continually to the people. They were given this time of grace and mercy so that they would have every opportunity to find salvation.

If God is holding you to certain commitments and constantly reminding you of their value, be pleased that He still has confidence in your ability to serve Him, but don't abuse His leniency and patience. Fulfill your personal mission.

For Perfect Timing

In the Old Testament we are told of how Joseph was put into a holding pattern. At the end of his incredible journey, his brothers were before him seeking forgiveness for what they had done to him earlier in life. Joseph had been sold into slavery and had been reported as dead. In Genesis 50 he said, "You meant evil against me, but God meant it for good in order to bring about this present result, to preserve many people alive."

There was a time for Joseph to become the Prime Minister of Egypt. But there was a time for him to sit in prison, too. Galatians 4:4 says, "But when the fulness of time came, God sent forth His son." For thousands of years the prophets and priests kept looking for the coming Messiah. They were in a holding pattern because God's timetable progresses as He ordains. After all, when it comes to time, He *is the Alpha and the Omega.*

For Teaching

Remember Naaman (2 Kings), the leper captain of the Syrian king? A little captive servant girl told him to go to her country to see Elisha the prophet. He went to Israel, where Elisha met him and told him to dip himself seven times in the muddy Jordan River.

Naaman became indignant and disgusted. He said he had pools back home where the water was pure and clean. Why should he want to go into the dirty Jordan River? Naaman had come to Israel thinking there would be some sort of miracle right there at Elisha's doorstep. He started to go back home.

A friend and traveling companion of Naaman's encouraged him to wait. Since he was already there, the friend observed, why didn't he just go ahead and give Elisha's suggestion a try? So, Naaman yielded. He dipped himself seven times in the Jordan. When he came up the seventh time, his flesh was like a newborn baby's. He was healed; completely cured.

Naaman had had preconceived notions about how Elisha was going to treat him, but his notions had been incorrect. After Naaman was healed, he said, "Now I know."

There's a lot of difference between what we think about something and what we later learn to *know* about it. Sometimes God teaches us lessons that we can only fully comprehend with time.

For Spiritual Growth

James 1:2-4 says, "Consider it all joy, my brethren, when you encounter various trials, knowing that the testing of your faith produces endurance. And let endurance have its perfect result that you may be complete, lacking in nothing." James tells us that trials can be used of God. You never get free of them until you learn from Him what He wants to teach you. Paul learned this in prison. Job learned it atop an ash heap. You can learn it wherever you are.

Yes, indeed, there are legitimate holding patterns. If you are making circles and not seeing growth, it could be because you are in a legitimate holding pattern. I don't want you to start feeling guilty if you are not currently sensing spiritual growth in your life. You may be growing incredibly, but by God's choice you are on hold. Talk to God regularly about your life. Strive always to know His will for you.

ILLEGITIMATE HOLDING PATTERNS

As we noted earlier, not all holding patterns are legitimate. God *does* want you to show progress in your Christian walk. If your holding pattern has been caused by your own decisions, then your timidity or laziness can be thwarting your witness and walk.

The Bible tells us of mankind's history of being "on hold" in his witnessing for God and service to Him. In Numbers 13 and 14 the nation of Israel sinned grievously and put itself into a locked holding pattern in relation to God's plan for the Jews.

I think there can be more lessons learned from those two chapters in Numbers about spiritual growth in a person's life than any other passage in the Old Testament. From my perspective, there were three reasons why the Jews found themselves locked into an illegitimate holding pattern which caused them to wander for forty years in the wilderness. By examining their errors, perhaps we can avoid such problems in our own lives.

The Jews Forgot Their Past

One of the chief reasons the children of Israel went into a holding pattern was that they forgot what God had done for them previously. In Numbers 14:3,4 they showed a lack of faith when the spies came back with a negative report about the Promised Land. The people cowered and cried out, "Let us go back to Egypt. Would it not be better for us to return? Let us get a new leader."

They wanted to go back to where they had been. They were content to regress. They had forgotten all that God had done for them. The God of yesterday was no longer sufficient for their current needs. Their faith was weak.

How well this should serve to remind us that yesterday's faith is not sufficient for today. We cannot rely on the past if we intend to grow in the future. We must feed and enhance our faith every day and nurture it through prayer and study.

I am amazed to think of what the Jews forgot in so short a time. Years had not passed since God had blessed them, merely a few days. How could they forget how God placed His hand on Moses? How could they forget the plagues? How could they forget Moses speaking before Pharoah and receiving permission to let the people go? How could they forget the passover? How could they forget the parting of the Red Sea? How could they forget the water they saw come from the rock?

How could they forget all these things? I can't explain it — I just know they did.

Today, we can be just as guilty and fall into just as serious a holding pattern if we forget what God has done for us. Is there anything more ungrateful than short memory of a God-given blessing?

The Jews Lost Their Initiative

Once confronted with some disheartening news, the children of Israel shrank back in fear. They became passive, depressed, defeated. In Numbers 14:2 they said, "Would that we had died in this wilderness."

Isn't that amazing? God had a land of milk and honey for them, and all of a sudden they decided they would rather wander around in the desert, or even die. That's often typical of our own lives as Christians, or our work as congregations. Instead of eagerly advancing to new conquests, we decide to sit and think. *Why grow,* we wonder? *Why expand? Why reach out? Why teach missions giving? Why increase church planting? Why witness to our home community? Let's be satisfied with the group we already have. We know everybody.*

So, we sing with gusto on Sunday morning, we're "standing on the promises" when, in truth, we'd rather just be "sitting on the premises."

I like the story about the congregation that needed to remodel its church, but had lost the initiative to undertake the project. The people didn't want to spend the money or put in the time required to make the repairs, even though their building was falling apart. They ignored the decay of the church until one day the chairman of the building committee was beaned on the head by some falling plaster. He immediately called a meeting of the building committee. The committee came up with four suggestions and presented them to the congregation:

1. We will build a new church.
2. We will build a new church on the same site as the old church.
3. We will use the materials of the old church to build the new church.
4. We will worship in the old church until the new church is built.

Upon hearing this series of recommendations, one senior saint in the church stood up and said, "In other words, if I'm hearing you correctly, we are going to stay in the same building and continue to repair and remodel it until we've got ourselves a new church. O.K., I'm for it. My only question, is, why didn't we just do that to begin with?"

Good question. Why *does* the roof have to fall in on us before we take some initiative?

The Jews Feared the Future

From their vantage point in the wilderness, the Jews felt they had a lot to be afraid of. They began to look out and see walled cities and giants and all the armaments the enemy had and they became frightened. Numbers 13:28 says, "The people who live in the land are strong." The spies had given a blood-chilling report: "The cities are fortified and very large; and moreover, we saw the descendants of Anak there. Amalek is living in the land of the Negev and the Hittites and the Jebusites and the Amorites are living in the hill country, and the Canaanites are living by the sea and by the side of the Jordan."

No one wanted any part of this situation. No one, that is, except two; Caleb and Joshua.

Caleb came forward and quieted the people. He shouted, "We should by all means go up and take possession of it, for we shall surely overcome it." Caleb was intent upon breaking the timid

Jews out of their holding pattern.

But the men who had been spies with him and Joshua said, "We are not able to go up against the people, for they are too strong for us. . . . The land through which we have gone, in spying it out, is a land that devours its inhabitants; and all the people whom we saw in it were men of great size."

That's some exaggeration. *All* the people they saw were "of great size.? Come on now, don't you think they saw a few babies over there? When people have a few problems, they really can exaggerate.

In verse 33: "There also we saw the Nephilim (the sons of Anak are part of the Nephilim); and we became like grasshoppers in our own sight, and so we were in their sight."

When you become like grasshoppers in your own sight, when you do not see yourself as you really are, especially in the power of God, what happens? You sell yourself short. Consequently, so does everyone else. Where was the God of Israel? Still there, of course, but not called upon by His people.

In Numbers 14:20, the result of the Jews' fear of the future and their complacency about the present and their forgetting of the past was that they went into a holding pattern. God was so sorely disappointed, He considered eliminating the race. But Moses prayed for a pardon, so the Lord said, "I have pardoned them according to your word."

Nevertheless, punishment was in order. "But indeed, as I live, all the earth will be filled with the glory of the Lord. Surely all the men who have seen My glory and My signs, which I performed in Egypt and in the wilderness, yet have put Me to the test these ten times and have not listened to My voice, shall by no means see the land which I swore to their fathers, nor shall any of those who spurned Me see it."

God put them into a holding pattern. For forty years the adults walked around in circles until they died. Only the children and Caleb and Joshua were permitted to enter the Promised Land.

There are some especially interesting things about this passage. It was their flesh that put the Jews into the holding pattern. Look at Numbers 14:4: "Let us appoint a leader and return to Egypt." They decided, in the flesh, to return to Egypt. When God told them He was going to put them in a holding pattern and keep them in the wilderness and keep them from their desire, it was their flesh that tried to get them out. After Moses told them they would wander in the wilderness, the people mourned greatly. But in verse 40 we read, "In the morning, however, they rose up early and went up to the ridge of the hill country, saying 'Here we are; we have, indeed, sinned, but we will go up to the place which the Lord has promised.' But Moses said, 'Why then are you transgressing the commandment of the Lord, when it will not succeed?'"

What a Scripture! They had made a choice and now they had to live with it for forty years. Illegitimate holding patterns are always products of the flesh.

Something else here is interesting. Notice that God had appointed Moses to lead them away from their problems, but they tried to appoint a leader to take them back. God will always give His people a leader. If they won't follow him, He'll let them select one of their own, but will leave them in the wilderness. He'll always put His hand upon someone and say, "This one is mine; I'm going to anoint and strengthen him." Too often the people try to select a leader not of God's choice. God says, "O.K., go ahead and appoint somebody. Select whomever you wish, but you will lose My best for you."

It's also interesting that the Jews mourned greatly when they heard the report of the spies. And they also mourned greatly when they heard that they had to stay in the desert. Isn't it ironic that they were sad when they had to go and sad when they had to stay? When God's people get into a holding pattern, they find themselves feeling unhappy no matter what the conditions are.

Only two Jews broke the holding pattern. We need to look at Joshua and Caleb and ask ourselves, "How did they get out of the holding pattern and how can we do the same?" I believe there are several answers to this question.

We Should Emulate Successful, God-honoring People

One of the ways Joshua broke out of the holding pattern the other Jews were in was by studying the actions and words of Moses carefully. Joshua became a serious pupil of his mentor. The Bible says, "Thus the Lord used to speak to Moses face to face, just as a man speaks to his friend. When Moses returned to camp, his servant, Joshua, the son of Nun, a young man, would not depart from the tent" (Ex. 33:11).

Joshua felt that Moses was a great man of God, ordained by

God. He determined to stay as close to that man as he possibly could. Joshua followed Moses the way the nursery rhyme lamb followed Mary: everywhere that Moses went, Joshua was sure to go. He wanted to be ready for Moses' mantle to fall on him one day. Joshua broke the normal pattern by leaving the crowd and focusing his attention on a man of God.

We can learn from this. By reading the Scriptures and emulating the lives of the apostles, we can lead more effective Christian lives. By attending Sunday school and church regularly, we can draw wisdom from our church elders. What we learn in these studies can make us more effective workers for God.

We Should Dare to Be Different.

Caleb had gumption. He was nobody's "yes man." When the crowd yelled for a return to Egypt, Caleb argued an opposite view. As the cowards demanded, "Retreat, retreat," Caleb announced that he was ready to go up and claim the land and drive off the heathen. Caleb dared to be different in a crowd. The crowd is always in a holding pattern. If you want to break the barriers, you're going to have to be different.

We Should Exercise Our Faith.

In Numbers 14 after the children of Israel decided to appoint a leader and go back to Egypt, verses 6 and 7 tell us about Joshua and Caleb. They spoke to the congregation and said, "The land which we passed through to spy out is an exceedingly good land. If the Lord is pleased with us, then He will bring us into this land, and give it to us."

Look then at verse 9. From saying, "*If* the Lord is pleased," they finished their exhortation by saying of the enemies, "Their protection has been removed from them, and the Lord is with us; do not fear them."

That's exactly what happens: When you begin to declare your faith in God, in spite of what the crowd is saying or doing, you'll increase in your determination to serve and represent Him. Joshua and Caleb did. By the time they ended their speeches, they were proclaiming the Promised Land as their own. What confidence!

We Should Possess a Different Spirit

If you are going to get out of your holding pattern, you're

going to have to be like Caleb and possess a different spirit. In talking to Moses, God said that the Children of Israel would have to stay in the wilderness because of their sin. Yet He added, "But My servant Caleb, because he has a different spirit and has followed Me fully, I will bring him into the land which he entered. . . ."

Caleb possessed a different spirit. Later (Joshua 14:7) we read that Joshua has become leader of the Jews and Caleb is set to take possession of his promised area. Caleb tells Joshua, "I was forty years old when Moses the servant of the Lord sent me to Kadesh-Barnea to spy out the land, and I brought word back to him as it was in my heart." Now, that's the key — *as it was in my heart.* You see, when Caleb was spying out the land, he saw a mountain. When he saw that mountain, a fire began to burn within him.

That is my mountain, Caleb thought. *That is my land. This is what God promised would be mine.* Now, at 85 years of age — old enough to be retired — Caleb looked at Joshua and said, "I am as strong this day as I was in the day that Moses sent me. . . . Now, therefore, give me this mountain" (Josh. 14:11,12, KJV).

When you begin to have that fire for God in your life and you begin to have that different spirit, it will make all the difference in the world. You will get out of the holding pattern.

When Noah's spirit was strong, he could resist the flood; when he lost his strong spirit, he couldn't even resist the wine flagon. When Samson's spirit was strong, he could win any battle; when he lost his strong spirit, he couldn't even control Delilah. When Saul's spirit was strong, he conquered the kingdom; when he lost his strong spirit, he couldn't conquer his own jealousy. When David's spirit was strong, he conquered the giant Goliath; when he lost his strong spirit, he couldn't control his own lust.

A different spirit. A cause. A purpose. A fire. Do you have a different spirit or are you locked into your old set behavior?

We Should Walk in the Power of God

When you want to get out of the holding pattern, you must have the power of God. If you turn to Deuteronomy 32, you will find the farewell address of Moses. Joshua has already been ordained the new leader of the Jewish people. Moses is not going into the Promised Land; he is set to go to Mount Nebo and merely to look at the land.

Moses was the man of the mountain. He watched the eagles as he climbed there. He noticed their characteristics. He noted how his relationship to God was like the baby eaglet's to its parent. God circles His children, protects them and cares for them. He feeds them, loves them, raises them, yet allows them freedom to spread their wings as their energies direct them.

Moses said God was "Like an eagle that stirs up its nest." God is a disturber. As those babies grow larger and stronger, He begins to flap His wings over the nest. He prods and challenges. He wants them to come out of the nest. He wants them to fly.

Moses also said, "He spread His wings and caught them, He carried them on His pinions." God is a deliverer. He develops us. He motivates us. And then He delivers us. He swoops under us with His everlasting arms and picks us up. God will take care of us.

God will never put more on us than we can handle, but He will challenge us with enough to enable us to grow. God has created us· to live beyond our means. Although this philosophy does not apply to financial management, it is completely appropriate to spiritual enhancement.

God is looking constantly for men and women to "break out" of self-imposed limitations and to accomplish what the world declares impossible. Why? Simple: so that we can encourage other believers to reach their God-given potential, too.

And that's a truth you can HOLD on to!

CHAPTER 4

Can
a Person Be Forgiven
Continually for the Same Sin**?**

Can a person be forgiven continually for the same sin? We will deal with this question as Paul did in Romans 6. When I was in college I especially enjoyed theology, and Romans was my favorite book. It's a book that confronts the question of sin head-on. I can think of no subject that deserves more time.

To begin to get a perspective on how God judges our sin, let me set the record straight. There is nothing you can do to make God love you more. Nothing. The flip side of that statement is, there is nothing you can do to make God love you less. God's love is unconditional. It is impartial. It is everlasting. It is infinite. It is perfect.

When I say there is nothing you can do to make God love you more, what I mean is that you cannot get "Brownie points" with God. You can do that in our society and perhaps even in your family. But it does not work with God. God's love for you and me is not based on our past, our potential, or our performance. God doesn't love a Christian more than He loves a non-Christian. There's nothing you or I can do that would make God love us more than He loves us right now. He has a perfect love.

It is also true that there is nothing we can do to make God love us less. That's very difficult for us to understand because in a human family many of the relationships that we build with one another are based on not hurting or displeasing anyone. God doesn't work that way. If we obey God, He loves us, and if we disobey God, He loves us. If we praise His name, He loves us; if we curse Him, He loves us. That's some love, isn't it? I don't understand it. I certainly can't match it. It's a perfect love for me. God's love is not dependent upon me. How true that is because God showed His love to sinners, such as us, by sending His Son to die for us. He did that while we were yet unlovely, while we were yet in sin, while we were willfully disobeying Him.

Now I think that by this point we understand that God's love is unquestioned. But God's love and God's desire are two different things. God desires that all men should come to repentance. In 2 Peter 3:9 we see, "The Lord is not slow about His promise." He is long suffering and patient. He is "not wishing for any to perish, but for all to come to repentance." That's God's desire.

Can a person be forgiven for continually committing the same sin? I think the answer is yes. But that's much too simple. No theologian would let you off with just a yes.

There's a hymn called *He* which has a phrase which goes, "Though sometimes it hurts, the way we live, He always says, 'I forgive.'" That's a nice song, but when I read Romans 6, I do not think Paul would want that sung right before he preached. My concern is not God and His faithfulness and His love. God is not fickle. God is faithful. I'm not worried about God's ability to forgive me for sin. When I ask myself the question, "Can I be forgiven for the sin?" I really need first to ask two deeper questions: Why would a true Christian continually want to sin? Is a person who continually commits the same sin truly born of God?

THE PROBLEM OF SIN

In the first two verses of Romans 6, Paul deals with the problem of sin. Notice how he opens with, "What shall we say then. . . ." It's obvious from his question that he's had a previous discussion on this matter. In Romans 5 he talked about the fact that we are under Adam (that is, under sin). In verse 20 Paul makes a statement that gives rise to this discussion in chapter 6: "Where sin increased, grace abounded all the more."

Now, as Paul often does in the book of Romans, he continued an argument with an imaginary opponent. The opponent, or the objector, has supposedly said, "Paul, you have just said that God's grace is great enough to forgive every sin." Paul has replied,

"That's true."

The objector then says, "You are, in fact, saying that God's grace is the greatest and most wonderful thing that has ever happened to mankind." Paul again says, "That's true." Then the objector says, "If God's grace is the greatest thing that has ever happened to mankind, and if where sin is present grace is even more present, why then can't we as believers continue to go on sinning? If grace abounds in the arena to a greater extent where sin is also rampant, then why as a believer in the Lord Jesus Christ don't we just continue to sin a lot so we can exhibit His grace more?"

That's the pertinent question Paul is responding to in Romans 6:1 when he says, "Are we to continue to sin?" You may want to underline the word "continue" in your Bible. That word is in the present tense. That doesn't mean just yesterday, but every day: yesterday, today and tomorrow.

This question presented in Romans 6:1 has elements of sound logic. After all, if God forgives our sins and He is faithful, which He is, and grace abounds around sin, then it's logical (in the Christian mind-set) to think, "Let us sin, who cares?" It's a natural question. There's not a person in this world who is not affected by temptation and who does not have the desire to sin.

There is nothing that amuses me more than to be around Christians who act as if they are never tempted by sin. I'm amazed at how they can say with a straight face that they are not affected by sin. They somehow go through the temptations of life and are never fazed. In truth, however, there's not one of us today who, in the last 24 hours, has not been tempted. It's a natural inclination for us to sense an appeal of sin. It's also a spiritual matter. You almost can look at the motives of the heart of the person who asked the question in Romans 5 and imagine him saying, "I not only want to give in to my fleshly desires but I want to exhibit the grace of God. I want to exhibit before my brothers how God really does forgive me. I want to prove that I'm not under law."

Now to this, Paul gives an absolute response. In Romans 6:2 he says bluntly, "May it never be!" In the King James Version it reads, "God forbid." I love the Phillips translation: "Oh, what a ghastly thought!" The New English Bible says, "No, no!"

Just as a mother says to a little two-year-old, breaking the law in the household, "No, no, don't do that!" Paul is saying to the Christian Jew, "No, no!"

We cannot afford to live in sin continually. Paul gives us the reason in the last part of verse 2. He asks a question which he answers with a question. "How shall we who died to sin still live in it?"

Let me tell you a little bit about death to sin. There are a couple of things he doesn't mean by that. When Paul says, "How shall we who died to sin still live in it?" He does not mean that as a Christian, I have reached a plane of living where I cannot sin. Paul doesn't mean that at all. If we reach the place, in living as a Christian, where we cannot sin, then there is no need for us to pray, "Lead us not into temptation." We couldn't be tempted if we couldn't sin. If we were tempted, we couldn't care. One common denominator about temptation is that it always brings before us something that is appealing. You have never been tempted to do anything that you didn't want to do or like to do.

I never in my life have been tempted to eat spinach. When I wake up at one or two in the morning I never have a great craving for the stuff. I'm sure you can't understand that, but I just never have hunger pangs for spinach. However, I will be truthful with you. There *are* times I want to eat German chocolate cake. Now, that is temptation. You see, you can only be tempted by what you like.

So, when Paul says, "How can we, who have died to sin, still live in it?" Paul is not saying we are going to get to a place in this world where we are not touched by the appeal of sin. He is also not saying that as a Christian I am continually dying to sin. Because when he says, "How shall we who died to sin, still live in it?" that "died" is in the aorist tense and means the past. In other words, Paul says that as a Christian you have died. It has already happened.

In Romans 5 Paul talked about being in Adam and being in Christ. In Adam we die, in Christ we live. When we are in Adam, we are depraved, sinful in our nature. When we are in Christ, we are forgiven. In fact, in 1 Corinthians 15:22 we read, "For as in Adam all die, so also in Christ shall we all be made alive." Paul is very clear and distinct in showing us the difference between being in Adam and being in Christ. Paul says that there is a great difference. To paraphrase Paul's words in Romans we can say, "How shall we who died in sin still be comfortable in it?" He says it is very difficult for the Christian to be comfortable in sin if he continues to wallow in it and live in it. Paul is the one who said, "Therefore if any man is in Christ, he is a new creature; the old things passed away; behold new things have come."

Paul is clear in his writings about the fact that a Christian is a new person. A new life. A new mind-set. A new goal. A new direction. A new heartbeat. A new love. In Adam, it's our nature to sin, just as in this world our nature is to breathe air. Paul says, in Christ it's our nature to not want to sin.

One afternoon my children had been watching television. Some youngsters had gotten hold of several pigs and had tried to put diapers on them. My daughter Elizabeth was telling me about it and just cracking up. "Dad, you should have seen those dirty, old, muddy pigs." It's the nature of a pig to go to the mud hole.

Paul, in Romans 6, is talking about the changed life, inwardly, that produces a change outwardly. He is not talking about an outward change. We can take that pig as an example. Take one dirty, filthy, muddy pig and clean him up. Wash him, soap him, and lather him. You gals could put some of that sweet-smelling stuff on him. We could put a ribbon around his neck and an earring in his ear. It wouldn't make any difference because as we let that pig out the door he would find the nearest mud hole. It's his nature. Paul says when we are in Adam that's exactly the way it is. We live in filthy sin. But when we're in Christ, we're not going to desire to continue to sin.

THE PURPOSE OF OUR SALVATION

In Romans 6:4 we read, "We too might walk in newness of life." That's the reason we are saved. We're saved to walk in newness of life. We're saved to glorify God and show to this world a Christian example.

In 1 Corinthians 6 there are two passages that talk about the lifestyle of a Christian and a non-Christian. The question is not are we, as Christians, going to fall into sin? The question is, as Christians, are we continually going to fall into that same sin? In 1 Corinthians 6:9, Paul begins to describe those who have an Adamic nature: "Or do you not know that the unrighteous shall not inherit the kingdom of God? Do not be deceived; neither fornicators [people who are sexually immoral], nor idolators, nor adulterers, nor effeminate, nor homosexuals, nor thieves, nor covetous, nor drunkards, nor revilers, nor swindlers, shall inherit the kingdom of God. And such were some of you."

Paul says that's the way we all used to live. That was BC —
before Christ. That was before my personal salvation. That was
before Christ came into my life and made me a new creature.
But. . ."You were washed, you were sanctified, you were justified
in the name of the Lord Jesus Christ, and in the spirit of our
God." Paul is saying it is impossible for us to be Christians and
to have the old kind of lifestyle.

Ephesians 5:3 is a passage of Scripture that inspires me to live
a life of holiness. "But do not let immorality or any impurity or
greed even be named among you, as is proper among the saints."
Paul isn't saying not to do it. He is saying, don't even let it be
named among you. Don't let your name be associated with it. See
verse 5: "For this you know with certainty, that no immoral or
impure person or covetous man, who is an idolater, has an inheritance in the kingdom of Christ and God. Let no one deceive you
with empty words." Paul says, don't let anybody tell you he has
an inheritance in the kingdom of God and that he is a child of
God if he is living that kind of a sinful lifestyle.

I remember sitting down with a fellow who professed to be a
Christian, who was living in continual sexual sin. I confronted
him and disciplined him through the Word of God. He kept talking
about the fact that he was under grace. I took him to these passages
of Scripture where Paul says we are not under grace. You have
either never been saved or somehow you have strained that relationship. Paul says those people will not inherit the kingdom of God.

The issue is this: The only reason we continually live in sin is
because we do not hate sin enough. If you continually are falling
into the same trap of sin, it is because you have not as yet
developed the hatred for sin that you should have. One of the
things that the new birth will do for you is develop a disgust in
your life for sin. Even as a Christian when you fall into sin, you
will want to get out of it. As a believer when you begin to fall,
you will say to yourself, "Hey, I don't belong here; I don't feel
comfortable here." My concern is not for the Christian who falls
and gets back up. My concern is for the person who seems to be
content in continually falling into the same sin.

Paul understands this quandary and gives us two pictures of
salvation in Romans 6:3-10 to help us deal with it. He provides
some visual aids to help us understand that it is impossible for a
Christian to go on living a lifestyle of evil.

Paul first talks about being baptized into Jesus Christ. I do not particularly believe that he is just specifically talking about water baptism. I think that just as when I put my hand up to the light and make a shadow on the floor, water baptism is a shadow of our baptism into Jesus Christ. It's not the hand but the shadow. It's a picture. It's the evidence of what has happened. There's no shadow if there's no hand. There's no baptism if there is no spiritual baptism into Jesus Christ.

When Paul uses the word "baptism," he is basically saying that when a believer is immersed into water, he is surrounded by water. He isn't observing it or floating on top of it; he's not partially in it, he is submerged in it. Paul says when we are submerged (baptized) into Jesus we are surrounded by Him. But it is impossible for us to be surrounded by Him and live a life of continual sin.

Paul not only gives us a picture of baptism, but in verse 5 he also gives us a picture of grafting and uniting. We become united with Christ. That word "united" is used in the sense of grafting a branch into a tree. Over a period of time, that branch, when grafted into the tree, not only receives nourishment from the trunk, it also becomes life to that tree. The grafting makes the branch function like a natural branch.

Paul says we are no longer in Adam. When Adam fell from grace I was grafted into him. I was baptized into him. I was sinful in my nature. I wasn't there when Adam committed the first sin, but I certainly was affected by it. We all were.

I was born a sinner. Paul explained that when Jesus died on the cross we weren't there, but we were affected by it. As His creatures and creations, when He died, we died. When He was buried, we were buried. When He arose, we arose. Spiritually, there is a connection. We are united in Christ. We are surrounded by Him.

How can we stop this continual sin process? Paul gives us a formula. It's found in Romans 6:11-14. This is what I call the presentation of ourselves. It has two simple steps. If you look at verse 11 you can see them. This marks the first time, as Christians, that the Romans were asked to do anything. This is the first exhortation given to the Christian body. Verse 11 gives two things to do:

1. Even so consider yourself to be dead to sin,
2. but alive to God in Christ Jesus.

First of all, Paul says we are to remember we do not have to obey sin. We're dead to it. We do not have to sin. You may say,

"Will I sin as a Christian?" Yes, there will be times you will fall short of God's expectations for your life. But you don't have to sin. It's not something you can't control. It isn't something that is forced upon you. You don't have to go through half the day as a Christian and all of a sudden think. . .well, have I done my sinning today? You do not have to come under that.

Paul tells us that as we were in Adam, slaves to sin, now as in Christ, we become servants of Jesus. God has power to enable us to be effective. We are not only to consider ourselves as dead to sin, but we are to consider ourselves also live to God in Christ Jesus. That is our power.

In Romans 6:12,13 we see step #1 repeated. It's the statement, we do not have to obey sin. Look at verse 12: "Do not let sin reign in your mortal body that you should obey its lusts, and do not go on presenting the members of your body to sin as instruments of unrighteousness." Now, Paul would not use the phrase "do not" if we could not help ourselves. Paul wasn't writing scripture to frustrate us. He says do not let sin reign. He's showing sin here as a volitional, willful act. It is something we consciously do.

God also gives us strength to consecrate ourselves to Him. This is how we overcome sin. Look at Romans 6:13,14: "Present yourselves to God as those alive from the dead, and your members as instruments of righteousness to God. For sin shall not be master over you, for you are not under law but under grace." This is a great passage of Scripture. The law says, if you and I do not live up to its standards, we're in trouble. The law says, this is the requirement, and if you don't achieve it, too bad.

Paul says, however, that we are under grace. Now what he is saying is this: When we become children of God we have to understand there are going to be times when we will fail. But don't become depressed if you sin. Do not become depressed over your short-comings. Paul is saying, take heart. You're under grace. You are a servant of the Lord's. Therefore, there is easy access to forgiveness of that sin.

The most important lesson I learned as a Christian occurred when I was seventeen. I received Christ and began to develop a strong relationship with Him. Up until that time I was in and out, up and down, not stable at all. But at seventeen I committed myself to Him in a total way. Three days later, out on the basketball court, we were playing in a scrimmage game, and I ran down the court and twisted my ankle. As soon as I twisted my ankle, I took God's name in vain. I'll never forget when one of my best friends leaned over and said, "I thought you were a Christian." Emotionally, I went down the tubes. I thought I had blown it.

As they packed my ankle in ice, all of a sudden it hit me that I was not under the law. True, I had sinned and had not done as I should have done, but I was under grace. So, at that very moment I just said, "Lord, forgive me. I did not want to commit that sin, it was an accident, it was part of my old nature coming back. Forgive me." I was forgiven. I knew it in my heart.

You are under grace, too. You are not under the law. If we are under the law, we might as well close up the book and go home. None of us will make it. Paul says that Christians must walk a fine line. The objective is to avoid sin in order to please God; however, when we do sin, we should not throw up our hands and quit but instead get back into fellowship with God. Grace provides that opportunity.

THE POTENTIAL OF SIN

In Romans 6:15, Paul again raises the question, "what then? Shall we sin because we are not under the law but under grace? May it never be!" Now, the question is not can we continually commit the same sin. It elevates it a little bit and the question becomes *shall* we continually commit the same sin? There is a choice here that we all need to make. Paul says no. He gives good reasons why we should not continue in sin.

To begin with, sin makes us its slave. God's desire is that we become free from sin. Paul says one of the reasons we don't sin is because it makes us its slave. We're either, Paul tells us, a servant of Christ's or a slave to sin. Paul adds that the main problem with sin is that it makes us more indebted every day. Isn't that true?

Let's say, for example, that you and I are talking and I get a little upset about what you say so I decide I'm going to commit a little bit of the sin of anger, and I make some cutting remarks. Not many, but enough. You look at me and think, he insulted me. So what do you do? You insult me right back. Then what do I do? I do a little bit more. It's the continual, downward process of sin.

Have you ever told a white lie? Then you have to cover up the white lie with another white lie. Afterwards the white lie that you used to cover the first white lie also needed to be covered.

Forty-two white lies later. . . . Well, that's what happens when we sin. It has the potential to keep dragging us down. It makes us its slave.

Another thing, sin makes us ashamed. In Romans 6:21 Paul says, "What benefit were you then deriving from the things of which you are not ashamed? For the outcome of those things is death." He's talking about shameful deeds that we'd like to forget. It might involve some hurtful words we'd like to pull back or the mending of some relationships that are strained because of sin. Whatever the sin has been, it causes us to feel embarrassed about it.

Finally, the worst consequence of sin is that it can kill us.

Do you remember when you were learning to ride a bicycle? When I was learning, I could do O.K. once I got going. As long as I kept pedaling, my balance was all right. I learned to balance before I learned to stop. I can vividly remember the stops. My ride was nice, but after awhile the ride had to stop. I can remember crashing into things like hedges, because that's the only way I knew to stop. I had this bike, I knew I had the brakes, I knew how to balance myself and how to pedal along, but I didn't know how to stop. I'd ride and crash, ride and crash. The brakes were there, but I didn't know how to use them.

Do you know what Romans 6 is for the believer? It's Paul giving you some "brakes" in the sin process of your life. Paul doesn't want Christians to excuse themselves for sinning, or to go around saying, "Well, grace abounds because I sin more." Don't rationalize your sin. Paul says in effect, "Look, I have given you some brakes in Romans 6. Use them." If there is any lesson we can learn from this passage, it would be the fact that God is faithful. Continual sin in a person's life should cause us to question if the person really is a true, born-again believer. The Christian does not have to sin. There is freedom from sin.

How Can I Know Where I Am Spiritually?

Chairs play an important part in our lives. Consider this question: "Which chair do you sit in?"

I think I first recognized the importance of chairs when I was three or four. In our family, as we sat around the table, we each had a specific chair to sit in. I knew there was a reason we sat in those special places. My father sat at the head of table; he was the spiritual leader in our home. My mother always sat in the chair that was closest to the kitchen. She had a servant's heart and needed to get up often since my brother and I had a knack for spilling milk. We also had a special chair for our guests, and it was placed so the guest would have a nice view out the window.

My father had a special chair in the living room that you could sit in except when he came in the room. It was kind of a lay-down, lay-back, let-me-read-my-book-and-kick-off-my-shoes chair. If we didn't get off, we were lifted off.

When I went to school I understood the importance of chairs there, too. In the reading class, three groups of chairs signified students of various reading levels. Wc also had a chair in the cloak room that I personally never visited. What I understood well was that if you didn't behave properly, the teacher would send you there for discipline.

In the fifth grade my teacher set up a judicial system to teach us law. We tried fellow members of the class. I was elected by the class to be the judge. I enjoyed that! That was the first time anyone made the criminal the judge! I sat in a special chair when I acted as judge.

The high school I attended had home rooms where we sat in alphabetical order. On the basketball team, those who started the game always sat closest to the coach. If you didn't play often, you sat further down. Where I sat on the bench was very important to me.

Chairs do have special significance. In this chapter we are going to consider three chairs. The first chair is marked "commitment." Sitting in that chair as a Christian signifies that you are committing your life to God, your family, and your church.

There is a terrific difference between the person who sits in chair number one and the person who sits in chair number two which is labeled "compromise." There is one question to consider continually: How is it that we, as individuals, or as a collective body, slide so easily from godliness to godlessness? It is common for people to go from chair number one to chair number two. How is it that our families can disintegrate so easily before our very eyes? How is it that a person, who at one time is hot, can begin to cool off spiritually?

There was a time in our lives when we really knew what we should be doing. Lately, however, we aren't so sure. There was a time in our lives when we said like Paul, "This one thing I do." But now we're just not as sure. Life has become diversified, splintered, complex.

Worse yet, it is very easy to slide on to chair number three which is labeled "conflict." It 's bad enough to sit in chair number two, straddling the fence, trying to make both God and Satan happy. But it's really terrible when you get into chair number three, because when you sit there, you really don't know what's happening. Your life is full of disillusionment and difficulty.

These three chairs represent three stages of life. Let me show you how they impact us in various arenas of life.

Let's consider educational institutions — Harvard, Yale and Princeton, the Ivy League schools. Did you know that in the beginning those schools were all Bible colleges? Let's talk about the slide from conservative, fundamental Bible teaching, Bible preaching and Bible living to liberalism. What causes that slide? At one time, the only major subject at the Ivy League schools was Bible. Every student who went to those schools took Greek.

Can you imagine Greek being a required course? It was!

Each student also signed a commitment to have daily devotions before class. Then one day the colleges decided not only to offer Bible degrees, but also law degrees. They brought in other subjects and very soon the emphasis on God began to slide. Mandatory chapel was cancelled, prayer was made optional, devotional commitments were forgotten, and Greek was made an elective class.

Let's talk about countries. I love English history and study it often. In the 1700s there were two men, John Wesley and George Whitefield, who came out of Oxford University. They were on fire for God. They had tremendous minds and solid convictions. They sat in chair number one: total commitment. They used this zeal to lead England back to God. England has not lived in/and nor experienced, such times since those years. Now the country is cold spiritually. As we Americans consider our spiritual heritage, we are quick to see that we, as a nation, have also slid right on down to chair number three.

Let's also consider the beginning of denominations. Why do denominations spin off from other denominations? Sometimes when the churches sit in the chair of compromise there is a spin-off because of coolness or disagreement. New groups break off and develop.

Remember, we always begin in chair number one. I want us to consider some of the characteristics of a person who sits in the chair of commitment.

To begin with, this is a person who has love. The church of Ephesus started in chair number one. In Ephesians 1:15 Paul said, "I heard of. . .your love unto all the saints" (KJV). In chapter 3 he says in effect, "I pray that you will be rooted and grounded in love and that you will know the love of Jesus Christ." In 4:16 he says that the church of Ephesus was literally building itself in love. In chapter 6, the very last verse, Paul says, "Grace be unto you who love our Lord Jesus Christ with a love that is incorruptible."

That is a beautiful benediction for any church. In that short book there are more references to the word "love" than anywhere else in the New Testament. You see, the church at one time sat right there in chair number one. Those New Testament church members had to have a committed love for their God because at times they had to forfeit their lives for Him.

Isn't it interesting that by the time we get to Revelation chapter 2, the same church is now compromising? That church, known

for its love, now is experiencing lukewarmness. When you leave
the glowing chair of committed love, you go to the mediocre chair of
lukewarmness. In Revelation 2 we read, "I know your deeds. . . .
But. . .you have left your first love" (vss. 2,4).

What happens when we leave our first love? What happens
when we leave that first chair? It is the same thing that happened
to the church at Laodicea in chapter 3 of Revelation. The first
thing that happens when we are lukewarm is that we make God
want to "spew us from His mouth." In Revelation 3:17 we read these
words: "Because you say, 'I am rich, and have become wealthy,
and have need of nothing,' and you do not know that you are
wretched and miserable and poor and blind and naked."

In chair number one we are spiritually sensitive, but in chair
number two we become spiritually insensitive. We are spiritually
aware in chair number one, but spiritually unaware in chair number
two. In chair number one we have a possession that makes us red
hot; in chair number two we have a profession without possession.
In chair number one we are spiritually alive; in chair number two
we are spiritually dead. Chair number one is the convictional chair;
chair number two is the conventional chair. Chair number one is
the chair that's "on fire"; chair number two is the chair that's "on
furlough." Chair number one is the one that lives for today and
has testimony of what God is doing *today;* chair number two lives
for *yesterday* and continually talks about the "good old days."

It's interesting to consider how the great churches in America
today are growing. During the last few decades, the only churches
that have shown great growth have been strong, fundamental, red-
hot, evangelistic churches. The liberal denominations are going
down fast. If they don't stop their attendance loss, by the year
2000 some won't even exist. Folks have decided that life is so
weighty and confusing they need to go to church where they can
find warmth, direction, Bible teaching and preaching. So, the
growing churches today are the ones sitting in chair number one.

We really have to feel sorry for the fellow who sits in chair
number three, labeled "conflict." In that chair, a person has moved
from love that was red-hot, to lukewarmness, to coldness. In this
chair we ask ourselves, "What happened to me? What happened
to my church? What happened to my family, who, at one time,
were sitting in chair number one?"

A few years ago I spoke at a cold, liberal church. The older
laymen asked if I would come to their church some Sunday to

preach. Understand that in this particular church there were people who sat in all three chairs. The older members who started the church were still committed to Jesus Christ and were still sitting in chair number one. They were interested in revival, evangelism and the things that really build a church. The pastor, however, sat in chair number two. And most of the new people sat in chair number three.

I didn't know any better and went in and preached a simple, red-hot message: "You must be born again." At the end of the service I asked people to raise their hands if they wanted to be born again. Of 250 people, probably 175 raised their hands. I thought they misunderstood me. So, I asked the same question again, but to make sure they understood, I asked them to stand. Again, 175 people stood. I had to pinch myself to make sure I hadn't died and gone to heaven. I thought, *Well, maybe they are still not quite understanding.* So again, I said, "If you really would like to receive Christ, please come forward." They all came. The preacher sat behind me, very disgusted, wondering to himself, *How did he get in here?* That's what the three chairs are like in church life.

Now, let's consider the three chairs in your family life. As an example of a family man we will consider King David. David was a beautiful example of a man whose commitment helped him set priorities. He was a man after the very heart of God. In Psalm 42:1 we read, "As the deer pants for the water brooks, so my soul pants for Thee, O God." That reminds me of brand new Christians who have just found Christ. They are eager. They feel that every time the church is open they should attend. They desire to read the Bible every day. They go out and witness whenever they can. They don't worry about delivery or technique. After we've been serving the Lord for so long, we get paranoid about it and think, *Well, I'd like to witness more but I don't know how to, properly.* And the longer we put it off, the more paranoid we become. There's nothing quite like an eager new Christian.

How does that relate to your family? Many of your parents sat in chair number one. There is a high probability that, as their child you will sit in chair number two. There is always the tendency to go from hot to cold; seldom from cold to hot. You don't climb up the hill as easily as you slide down the hill. In chair number one, the person usually attends both services: Sunday morning and evening. It's not a big chore for them to come Sunday night. They just happen to truly love the Lord Jesus.

The people who sit in chair number two come on Sunday mornings. The person in chair number one attends church because he wants to; the person in chair number two attends church because he "ought" to. In chair number one, the person is priority-oriented; in chair number two, he or she is pleasure-oriented. In other words, they come to church if the church "has something good" for them. They check the schedule to see who is preaching and then decide if they will come.

David sat in chair number one. Where did David's son sit? Solomon sat in chair number two. It happens many times. David wanted to build the temple for God. Solomon wanted to build palaces for himself. If you really want a good study, look into Ecclesiastes 2:1-11 and you'll find forty-six personal pronouns which imply that Solomon was working for himself:

> I said to myself, "Come now, I will test you with pleasure. So enjoy yourself." And behold, it too was futility. I said of laughter, "It is madness," and of pleasure, "What does it accomplish." I explored with my mind how to stimulate my body with wine while my mind was guiding me wisely, and how to take hold of folly, until I could see what good there is for the sons of men to do under heaven the few years of their lives. I enlarged my works: I built houses for myself; I planted vineyards for myself; I made gardens and parks for myself, and I planted in them all kinds of fruit trees; I made ponds of water for myself for which to irrigate a forest of growing trees. I bought male and female slaves, and I had homeborn slaves. Also I possessed flocks and herds larger than all who preceded me in Jerusalem. Also, I collected for myself silver and gold, and the treasure of kings and provinces. I provided for myself male and female singers and the pleasures of men — many concubines. Then I became great and increased more than all who preceded me in Jerusalem. My wisdom also stood by me. And all that my eyes desired I did not refuse them. I did not withhold my heart from any pleasure, for my heart was pleased because of all my labor and this was my reward for all my labor. Thus I considered all my activities which my hands had done and the labor which I had exerted, and behold all was vanity and striving after wind and there was no profit under the sun.

Solomon was pleasure-oriented whereas David, his father, was priority-oriented. What happens in your family when someone gets to chair number three? Who sits there? Rehoboam, David's grandson, sat in chair number three. He was the last king of Israel because he made such a mess out of it, he caused the kingdom to divide. A trait of the person who sits in chair number three is perplexity.

He just doesn't know what's happening.

Many times I have seen adults whose parents sat in chair number one, they sit in chair number two and now they look at their child sitting in chair number three and wonder, "What in the world happened?" I'll tell you what happened. If I'm in chair number three I'm all messed up. And the reason I'm all messed up is because I can't see chair number one where grandpa or grandma sat. Instead, all I see is chair number two. Chair number two people go to church but they don't thoroughly love God. Chair number two people bring Bibles to church, but when they go home they put them back on the shelf and don't pick them up until next Sunday morning. Chair number two people, when called on to pray, can stand up and pray. But they won't pray in the home with the family or lead family devotions. It's just a Sunday thing. Chair number two people just know "Sunday stuff." Nothing else. The child in chair number three looks at his parents, in chair number two, and calls them hypocrites.

Let's take Abraham as another example. Abraham sat in chair number one. God told him to get up and go, and he went. He was sold out, ready to move out and to be obedient to God. When you follow Abraham throughout the early books of the Bible you will find that each time Abraham arrived somewhere the first thing he did was build an altar to the Lord. The second thing he did was to give praise to God. The third thing he did was to dig a well. His son's name was Isaac. Isaac sat in chair number two. There is one interesting characteristic about Isaac. When Isaac moved to a new area, he dug a well. And then, sometimes he built an altar, and sometimes he didn't. See what began to happen? In Abraham's life it was God first, sustenance second. With Isaac it was sustenance first, God second. Isaac moved into the second chair.

Abraham was right with God. In chair number two where Isaac sat, he "looked" like he was right with God. He had been around long enough to be able to walk the walk and talk the talk and sing the songs. He really looked the part. But if you watched him closely, you discovered he was role playing.

Let's look next at Jacob, the grandson of Abraham, the son of Isaac. He was in chair number three. He was a cheater, a con artist, a deceiver who tricked even his own father. The pattern held true to form once again.

We could also put Joshua in the first chair. In Judges chapter

2 we find all three phases. Judges 2:7 says, "And the people served the Lord all the days of Joshua, and all the days of the elders who survived Joshua." This could be said of the people who live in chair number one: They know God — they know the works of God. In verse 10 we read, "And all that generation were gathered to their fathers." The people who sit in chair number two know *about* the works of God. In other words, there was a group of people who hadn't seen the walls of Jericho fall. But they had heard *about* them. They knew God, but only *about* His works. Then the Word says that there was another generation, after that, who did not know God, nor did they know the works of God. That's chair number three. As soon as that verse is completed verse 11 says, "They the sons of Israel did evil in the sight of the Lord." They neither knew God nor did they know about the works of God. And immediately they ruined their lives.

What are our comparable circumstances today? Well, first, we should identify which chair we sit in so that we can know where we are spiritually. Having read this chapter, you no doubt have already recognized which chair you most readily seem to fit into.

Additionally, we must keep in mind that the Bible and history teach us that there is a tendency for new generations to slide down to lower chairs. That tells us that if today we are in chair number one, the tendency tomorrow will be for our children to wind up in chair number two. But even more disturbing to us as parents should be the realization that if we sit in chair number two, there is a high probability that our children will sit in chair number three. That's where the problem lies.

If you ask, "How can I keep my children in chair number one?" focus on these four words:

"Example" — The better Christian example you are for your family, the better your chance will be of keeping your children in chair number one.

"Environment" — The better Christian environment you keep your family in, the better will be your chances of not having your family slide.

"Experiences" — The better the Christian experiences are that you give your children, the more reserve in the bank they will have when they need additional spiritual resources.

"Examination" — Examine yourself frequently, and ask yourself which chair you are seated in. It would be ridiculous for me as a parent to sit in chair number two, looking right but not always being right, and to expect my children to sit in chair number one. After all, it would be foolish for me to expect my children to attend Sunday school and church in the morning and evening, if I didn't. It would be folly for me to expect my children to put God first as they grow up, seeing that I didn't allow God first place in my time, possessions and tithe. Wouldn't it be ridiculous to expect a level of living from my kids that I don't personally display before them? Kids don't go up on their own, they only go down on their own.

The good news is that you don't have to stay in chair number two or three. You may be there now, but you don't have to remain there. Change chairs! Decide that the life you are now living is not the life you want to be living. Get out of chair number two or three and say, "As for me and my house, we are going to sit ourselves down in chair number one and live committed Christian lives."

Revelation 2:5 presents us with the three *R*'s of success as a Christian:

REPENT — Turn your back on sin, and get rid of those things that are hindering your Christian life.

REMEMBER — Remember those good days when you walked close to God and had fellowship with him every day.

[RE]-DO — The Word says to do the first works again. Take action on your commitment!

Did you ever play the game musical chairs? You sit in a circle of chairs and when the music plays you get up and walk around the chairs. Everybody moves around the chairs waiting for the music to stop. When it does, you sit down. But there was one catch to the game. The moment the music stopped you had better find a chair quickly, because there is one less chair than there are people each time.

The whole point of the illustration is that there is a certain time in life to change chairs. That not only works in the kiddy games, but also in our everyday life. There is a certain time for moms and dads, boys and girls, grandmas and grandpas to change chairs. And the time to change chairs is *now* if God's spirit is speaking to you and telling you that you are in the wrong chair. Offer a prayer: "God, with your help at this moment I make a commitment to sit again in chair number one."

CHAPTER 6

What Should the Christian View of Divorce Be?

Divorce is one of the most talked about and controversial subjects within the Christian community. It is difficult to deal with because it affects so many people. Very few Christian families have not experienced a divorce among relatives and close friends. Because we love these people, we find it hard to scold or upbraid them for their sin. In fact, we don't know how to relate to them. It's very difficult to be righteously judgmental, biblical, and dogmatic while balancing that with grace, love, and Christian compassion.

People getting divorced always see themselves as exceptions to the rule. It's difficult to accept biblical teaching if experience seems contrary to it. We would rather take our human views and match them to biblical teaching. It's much easier to say what I am, and then find something in the Word of God to substantiate it. But that's game playing (and poor theology).

Nothing has destroyed the credibility of the church as much as divorce. Obviously, I am addressing divorce from a Christian perspective. I'm not talking about the world with its problems. I'm talking about us, the redeemed people of God.

In 1960, 2.9 million people were divorced. In 1980, 10.8 million people were divorced. But while the population has risen 30 percent, the divorce rate has risen 300 percent.

My focus in this chapter is on divorce in the Christian community. How are we going to handle this issue? During the twenty years that the world divorce rate increased 300 percent, the divorce rate in the church has increased by 600 percent. We're winning the wrong race. Now, obviously, that isn't numerical — it is a percentage — but before the 1960s you hardly heard of divorce in the church.

Divorce *used* to be a problem of the world. When divorce wasn't in our churches, we weren't confused about it. We really understood the issue. But when it began to happen within our own ranks, all of a sudden it became a cloudy issue. It is not because God's Word has changed. It's because, as Christians, our way of life and the Word of God are not meshing.

VIEWS OF DIVORCE

There are those who say that for no reason should anyone be divorced or be allowed to remarry. That's the ultra-conservative, legalistic viewpoint. Then there are those who can accept divorce under certain circumstances, but are against allowing the divorced person to remarry. Another view is that just as certain circumstances allow for an acceptable divorce, so do certain circumstances allow for an acceptable remarriage. And, finally, there are some who believe there is nothing wrong with divorce and remarriage for any reason.

Now our task is to determine which of these statements is the biblical viewpoint. I'm not interested in your viewpoint. You shouldn't be interested in my viewpoint. We should only be interested in what God's view is on this subject.

In 1981 scholars around the world met at Grand Rapids, Michigan, for three days and read long papers on marriage, divorce and remarriage. Probably the greatest theologians who have ever been assembled on that subject were there, and the only conclusion they could come up with is that they could not agree. Now if they spent three days and could not agree, I'm not naive enough to think I'm going to be able to give you, in a few pages, a pat answer that will completely satisfy all your questions. I do want you to understand this: If you do not agree, make sure your conclusion is based on biblical grounds, not your experience. Our disagreement must not be over your good marriage or your bad marriage. We must stick strictly to the Word of God in this matter.

We'll approach this subject with three questions: (1) How should things be? (2) What could things be? and (3) What happens when should and could don't blend?

HOW SHOULD THINGS BE?

In Matthew 19:8 Jesus explained how things should be in a Christian marriage. The Pharisees and the scribes came to the Lord and mentioned that Moses said if a man's wife has behaved indecently, the husband could write out a bill of divorce and let her go. Jesus said, "Because of your hardness of heart, Moses permitted you to divorce your wives; but from the beginning it has not been this way." Note the phrase, "But from the beginning it has not been this way." In other words, the original blueprint that God had for marriage was very simple and clear. Divorce was not in the picture when Adam and Eve were created in the image of God. It was one husband and one wife together for life.

But we also have to understand that in the beginning there was no sin. In Genesis 5:1, we read, "In the day when God created man, He made him in the likeness of God." In other words, when God created Adam and Eve, He made them like Himself. Perfect. Sinless. Then sin entered the world, and Genesis 5:3 says, "When Adam had lived one hundred and thirty years, he became the father of a son in his own likeness, according to his image." What happened? Adam and Eve were made in God's likeness. Seth, Cain, and Abel were made in the likeness of Adam. Sin had been brought into the human family.

So, when we were born, we were born with sin in our lives. Romans 5:12 tells us that. "Therefore, just as through one man sin entered into the world, and death through sin, and so death spread to all men, because all sinned." We've all come under that sin umbrella. When I was born into this world, I was born a sinner. Dad was a preacher, Mom was a Sunday school teacher, and I was a sinner. So sin messed up the ideal marriage. Now things aren't as they should be.

I received a note from a member of my congregation who knew I was going to write on this subject. It said, "Just a thought to illustrate that divorce was probably not in God's original plan. When he created Adam and Eve, he *didn't* create Adam and Eve and Josephine, just in case Adam and Eve didn't make it. Nor did he create Adam and Eve and Albert, for Eve's sake. God provided no alternatives, just one woman and one man."

Somebody told me that Adam and Eve really had it made. Adam didn't have to hear about all the other men that Eve used to date. And Eve didn't have to hear about Adam's mother's cooking.

WHAT COULD THINGS BE?

There's a possibility, even in a sin-cursed world with a society that no longer works out its problems, that you can still have a good, strong Christian marriage. There are certain conditions for a good Christian marriage, however.

To begin with, Christians are supposed to marry other Christians. There are no exceptions. Note 2 Corinthians 6:14-18. Read especially verse 14 where Paul talks about the danger of being unequally yoked, a believer with an unbeliever. This message needs to be taught and preached to the church continually. Begin at verse 14: "Do not be bound together with unbelievers; for what *partnership* have righteousness and lawlessness, or what *fellowship* has light with darkness? Or what *harmony* has Christ with Belial, or what has a believer in *common* with an unbeliever? Or what *agreement* has the temple of God with idols? For we are the temple of the living God; just as God said, 'I will dwell in them and walk among them; and I will be their God, and they shall be my people. Therefore, come out from their midst and be separate,' says the Lord."

If you are a Christian, you are not to marry a non-Christian. That's simple. Notice the word "partnership." Paul says that if a believer and an unbeliever are forced together, they can't have a partnership. They won't have the same goals. Notice the word "fellowship." What mutual joy will result from being unequally yoked? Notice "harmony." The unequally yoked couple will not have the same love. Concerning the word "common," they won't have the same interests. In "agreement"" they won't have the same philosophy.

Paul is saying about a believer and an unbeliever living together in marriage, "It won't work."

God's Word says it is wrong for a born-again, redeemed Christian to marry an unbeliever. Some Christians try to exempt themselves from this directive. I've heard all kinds of rationalizations for unequally yoked marriages. I hear, "Oh, I'm going to win him to Jesus." Maybe you will, but maybe you won't. That is not God's plan for evangelism.

As a pastor, I will not personally participate in a wedding ceremony for a believer and an unbeliever. I will marry two unbelievers. I'll give them Christian counseling first. I'll do everything I can to win them to Christ. And, of course, I'll marry two believers. To marry a believer and an unbeliever would just be helping them participate in something that God says not to do. I can't be part of that. When it comes time for you to be part of a wedding of a believer and an unbeliever, you literally and figuratively shouldn't "stand" for it.

A Russian proverb says, "When going to war, pray once. When going to sea, pray twice. When getting married, pray three times." It's hard to give you guidelines for a good marriage. I've seen marriages that I thought were going to be great, and only a few years later they weren't what I thought they would be. Others that I would not have given a chance to make it are now doing great. Marital maintenance is something we all handle differently, I suppose. Those who turn it over to God for direction amaze us all at how well they succeed.

I believe there are certain procedures Christians can follow. These will do much to help establish a marital relationship that will not end in divorce. First, people should pray about the challenges they will face in married life. God is eager to provide helpful advice. In James 1:5 we are told," If any of you lacks wisdom, let him ask of God, who gives to all men generously and without reproach, and it will be given to him."

I also recommend Christian counseling and testing so that character traits can be revealed, shared and discussed. A pastor can also share the biblical plan for marriage and can answer most questions one may wish to ask about money, sex, child care, family devotions, and spouse responsibilities. When two sweethearts begin to discuss their duties, their restrictions, and their obligations, much of the glassy-eyed, lovey-dovey behavior is replaced by a dose of reality. And that's good.

When Marriages Start Slipping

Your Christian marriage will begin to get in trouble if one partner loses interest in spiritual matters. If you're both not in the Word or in prayer, you stop discussing the things of God. The result? No longer does Ephesians 5 have any power over your marriage. Wives are not going to be submissive to their husbands, as they are to the Lord, if they're not walking with God. That has no relevance to them at all. Husbands aren't going to love their wives as Christ loved the church.

Once in awhile I'll run into a guy who will say, "I'll tell you right now, my wife did this and I'm not going to forgive her until she shows me she is repenting." I say to him, "Wait a minute," and tell him that if he loves his wife as Christ loved the church, he'll go the second mile, and the third mile. That's not being a doormat. There should be an awful lot of grace and forgiveness in any marriage. You may say, "But I've got rights, scriptural rights!" Who cares about rights? Jesus on the cross had rights, too. You've been listening to the world too much. The highest authority on marriage and divorce is not a divorce attorney — thank the Lord! They're making money off of people's misfortunes. Listen to God, not your local, would-be Perry Mason. You must accept God's word as your standard.

Turn to your Bible and let God settle the issue for you. When is divorce wrong? Jesus indicates that divorce without grounds of sexual immorality is wrong. In other words, he says to the Christian, "You can't divorce your partner for random reasons." You can't put the "incompatibility" sign up. It may work in court, but in Matthew 5:32 we read, ". . .I say to you that everyone who divorces his wife, except for the cause of unchastity, makes her commit adultery; and whoever marries a divorced woman commits adultery."

Divorce is wrong for you if your unbelieving spouse wants to make your marriage work. If he or she wants to stay with you, you should do so according to 1 Corinthian 7:12,13: "But to the rest I say, not the Lord, that if any brother has a wife who is an unbeliever, and she consents to live with him, let him not send her away. And a woman who has an unbelieving husband, and he consents to live with her, let her not send her husband away." Just because you are married to an unbeliever does not mean you have grounds for divorce — for yourself — as long as that unbeliever really wants to make that marriage work.

WHEN IS DIVORCE NOT WRONG?

Divorce itself is not sin. I'll give you examples of that. Jesus said that if there is sexual immorality it is not wrong for a Christian to divorce a mate. If an unbeliever walks out of your home, out of your marriage, Paul tells us in 1 Corinthians 7:15, "Yet, if the unbelieving one leaves, let him leave; the brother or sister is not under bondage in such cases but God has called us to peace." God Himself wrote out a bill of divorce in Jeremiah 3:8. Remember when Israel continually had committed spiritual adultery and God got fed up? He said, "I'm going to divorce you." Now if God, the sinless one, could write out a bill of divorcement, divorce *in itself* is not wrong.

Let me give you a word of caution here. We get on dangerous ground when we try to figure who the innocent party is in a marriage break-up. As a young pastor I decided that I would remarry people. . .under extreme circumstances. When I made that decision I thought I would be able to figure out who the innocent party was. I thought I could bring in both the husband and wife and ask them about their background. Much to my amazement, when I talked to the wife she was the innocent one. And when I talked to the husband, he was the innocent one. I found out they were both innocent! I found out that it was very difficult to judge. The more obvious offense is not necessarily the greater one. Marriage is like a tapestry. It is woven together, but all of a sudden it can fly loose and unravel. Many times an unraveling relationship that neither you nor I know anything about can cause one spouse to leave. There is sin in both lives.

Another statement I'll make is this: In most cases, when there is a divorce in a home, both parties have allowed sin to creep into their lives. I say that with love and kindness. In most cases that has happened. When there is divorce there is usually unforgiveness on both sides. Maybe one spouse went out and really committed sexual immorality so the other one is the innocent one. But there may be a time of repentance in this area of marriage that needs to be dealt with.

WHAT HAPPENS WHEN SHOULD AND COULD DON'T BLEND?

We know we should have an ideal marriage. But sometimes sin comes in and our marriage suffers. God's grace is sufficient for us. Perhaps you'll say that you have messed up one, or two, or even three marriages and you wonder what you should do now. There's a wrong question and a right question. "Is it lawful to divorce and remarry?" is the wrong question. That's the pick-up-a-stone-and-let-'em-have-it attitude. It's the eye-for-an-eye- and-a-tooth-for-a-tooth attitude. Jesus dealt with that. Remember when He wanted to heal the man on the Sabbath who had the withered and? He had just finished teaching the Pharisees that He honors mercy more than sacrifice. Those men didn't know anything about mercy and grace. They just knew about sacrifice and rules and regulations.

Jesus healed the man, and the Pharisees jumped all over Him saying, "It's not lawful to work on the Sabbath." He looked at them and asked them if they had an animal in the ditch would they pull it out? What He was teaching was this: The law can never stand on its own. The law of the Word has a foundation of grace underneath it.

The right question is, "How can I heal a broken relationship?" Too many of us have already made terrible mistakes. We need some love, care, and compassion. We don't need any rocks thrown at us. We don't need any "thou shalts"" or "thou shalt nots." What we need is for somebody to be loving and kind and understanding. Justice says we get what we deserve. Mercy says we don't get all that we deserve. Grace says we get all that we don't deserve. The law says the wages of sin is death, but grace says the gift of God is eternal life. The law says that the man who sins shall die, but grace says Jesus has come to give you everlasting life. The law says we demand holiness, and grace says we give holiness.

I think in Christian marriages there is only one difference between people who have marriages going and those who have given up. Those who have marriages going, in most cases, have problems as big as the ones that exist in marriages that have been given up on. Those who keep their marriages going find a way to appropriate God's grace for their problems. Those who give up on their marriages are those who give up on grace in the framework of marriage and family.

Perhaps you've been divorced and remarried; remember God loves you and has grace for you. In John 3 Jesus dealt with a respected teacher in the synagogue. In John 4:4 there is an interesting statement: "And He had to pass through Samaria." Do you know why He *had* to go through Samaria? Because there was a woman there who needed Christ. She had been married five times. If I were to preach on that subject I would say, "How Jesus Dealt With a Five-Time Divorced Woman." At the well outside of town, He talked to her about living water. She had a thirst for it, and she ran back into her village telling everyone to come see a man who told her everything she had ever done. The only difference between Jesus and others was that Jesus had grace for that lady.

Those people knew what she had done. She, no doubt, was the talk of the town. They came to hear Jesus, and the whole town was saved. Do you realize who was the first full-time mass evangelist? It was a five-time divorced woman. Brothers and sisters, that is grace.

To the Christians I say this: There are no easy answers. We need to uphold the biblical standard. We need to hold firmly in one hand the Word of God and what it says, but in the other hand we need to have a hand of compassion, care, love, and mercy that draws people in. To the person who has experienced one or more messed up marriages, the good news is this: If Jesus could use a five-time divorced lady there is never a place in your life where God's grace can't forgive, restore and use you, too, for His glory.

CHAPTER 7

What Is the Christian Stance Regarding Remarriage?

In this chapter, two questions will be faced. The first is, "When is remarriage permissible?" The second is, "When is remarriage *not* permissible?" God's Word allows remarriage under certain conditions. Most Christians believe that remarriage is permissible when the marriage and divorce occurred prior to salvation. We need to see what the Bible says about those who have not been privileged to sit under the sound teaching and direction of the Word, or to be in a Christian environment and atmosphere.

We realize the world has an entirely different set of priorities. Although people violate God's laws many times, many folks don't even realize what they are violating. Surely, divorce and remarriage are not pleasing to God. The church should not condone divorce or approve it. However, in the non-Christian setting, marriage is quite different from what it is in the church setting.

Paul said in 2 Corinthians 5:17, "Therefore, if any man is in Christ, he is a new creature — the old things passed away; behold, new things have come." Now when Paul said that old things are passed away, he even meant that bad marriages were erased by the redemptive blood of Christ. Sinners become new people. In fact, the word "new" in the original language means "that which is unaccustomed or unused, not new in time, not recent, but new as to the form or the quality."

Phrased another way, we have a different or new nature that

is contrasted to the old nature. When Paul says that in Christ we have a new nature, he is saying we've not become a new person in the fact that we look different, or that we change our name or outward appearance, but we have become new inwardly. We have a fresh start; a new start; a new opportunity. In God's eyes, all those things which have gone on in the past are forgiven and forgotten. They are not held against us.

Obviously, some of the sins we committed in our sinning days will continue to haunt us after we've received Christ. Receiving Him doesn't mean that the bad marriage or the mistakes we made before becoming Christians will no longer cause us problems. It isn't that easy. Sin has lasting consequences. But what it does mean is that in God's sight we are new creatures. If we've committed murder before being saved, we may still have to pay the penalty for that murder, but in God's eyes we are free from guilt through the blood of the Lord Jesus Christ.

If before you were saved you had a terrible problem with lying but now that you know Jesus you are no longer telling lies, you are a new person. If you committed adultery before being saved, when you come to the Lord Jesus, He forgives you. You may pay the penalty for those sins, but you are a new person — fresh, lily-white in the sight of God. That's forgiveness. That's pure grace.

The problem is that people aren't forgiving the way God is. God can forgive and totally forget. But sometimes in our human perspective we have a more difficult time with that. This word "new" that Paul uses is the same word Jesus used when He looked at His disciples and said, "Behold, I give you a new commandment." It's the same word Paul uses in Ephesians 2:15 when he speaks of the "new man" and in 4:24, "the new self." It's the same word John used in the book of Revelation when he said that there is a new heaven and a new earth and we have a new name written down. When Paul says we are new creatures in Christ Jesus, he means that in the eyes of the Lord, through grace, we no longer have to pay the price for the sins we've committed. We are totally forgiven.

People come to me quite often and say they regret their past lives. I understand that. But we have to understand, too, that redemption is total. Sometimes I hear church leaders talk about what people have done before their salvation. They infer that God will forgive murder and all kinds of horrible sins, but they never seem to imply that people who have had marriage problems qualify for equal forgiveness. I have good news for you. Divorce is not the unpardonable sin. You can be forgiven.

Ephesians 2:1 says, "And you were dead in your trespasses and sins, in which you formerly walked according to the course of this world, according to the prince of the power of the air, of the spirit that is now working in the sons of disobedience." No wonder people have problems in the world. "Among them we, too, all formerly lived in the lusts of our flesh, indulging the desires of the flesh and of the mind, and were by nature children of wrath, even as the rest." Now look at Ephesians 2:4-7 where the picture begins to change: "But God, being rich in mercy, because of His great love with which He loved us, even when we were dead in our transgressions, made us alive together with Christ (by grace you have been saved), and raised us up with Him, and seated us with Him in the heavenly places, in Christ Jesus, in order that in the ages to come He might show the surpassing riches of His grace in kindness toward us in Christ Jesus."

Then Paul says in verses 19-22, "so then you are no longer strangers and aliens, but you are fellow citizens with the saints, and are of God's household, having been built upon the foundation of the apostles and prophets, Christ Jesus Himself being the cornerstone, in whom the whole building, being fitted together is growing into a holy temple in the Lord; in whom you also are being built together into a dwelling of God in the Spirit." Regardless of your problems before salvation, if you have received Christ as personal Savior, you are part of the family of God. You have an inheritance; you are rich in mercy; you are rich in grace; you are God's child; you are going to go to the same place the rest of the redeemed go when we die, and you are going to be with Jesus. You're forgiven.

SEXUAL IMMORALITY

When one mate is, or has been, unwilling to repent and live faithfully with the other marriage partner, the faithful spouse is free. In Matthew 19:9 Jesus says, ". . .whoever divorces his wife, except for immorality, and marries another woman commits adultery."

Now that is a simple statement. That's not difficult to understand. Sometimes we try to take biblical truth and make it what it really is not. A principle I try to follow in interpreting the Bible is that if the normal sense makes good sense, seek no other sense. Sometimes I think we take simple passages and try to build into them an incredibly complicated interpretation. Jesus simply says that divorce and remarriage are permissible when there is proof of immorality.

Let's look at that word "immorality" for a moment. That comes from the Greek word "pornea" which is a word for pornography. It means illicit sexual activity. But it means more than that. It means illicit sexual activity as a lifestyle.

I want you to note a couple of things. We are not speaking about the mate who goes out and messes up his or her life with a quick lapse into sexual immorality but then comes home, repents, and keeps himself right after that. We are talking about a person who continually falls into a wrong sexual relationship outside the marriage union. What the Lord is trying to teach us here, I think, is the fact that we have to look at the person who is committing this sexual sin and determine in our mind whether or not this is going to be the lifestyle of that person. If so, the faithful spouse is free to divorce.

I will not argue that if one's mate goes out and has a sexual experience with someone that one doesn't have grounds for divorce. I will say, however, that it would be wonderful if there could be forgiveness. Wouldn't it be great if there could be understanding? It will hurt, of course. It takes time to go through the process. But wouldn't it be something if the forgiveness of our Lord could be transmitted through the person who was the "innocent party"? I would have you note that when Jesus said the innocent party has grounds for divorce, it was not a command. Jesus did not command you to leave your marriage partner if he or she has been unfaithful to you. He just said that it is an option for divorce.

A MATE'S DESERTION

Believer/unbeliever marriage is dealt with in 1 Corinthians 7:12-15: "But to the rest I say, not the Lord, that if any brother has a wife who is an unbeliever, and she consents to live with him, let him not send her away. And a woman who has an unbelieving husband, and he consents to live with her, let her not send her husband away. For the unbelieving husband is sanctified through his wife, and the unbelieving wife is sanctified through her believing husband; for otherwise your children are unclean, but now they are holy." That doesn't mean that the unsaved mate is saved. What it does mean is that that family or that mate is specially set apart. A special grace is apparent to that unsaved mate. The odds are a lot higher for that mate to become a Christian, and for those kids to become Christians, than if that marriage would break up.

Note again 1 Corinthians 7:15: "Yet if the unbelieving one leaves, let him leave." Notice that it doesn't say a mate was forced out, but rather that he or she left willingly. Don't kick a mate out of the home and then say, "Well, he left." "Yet, if the unbelieving one leaves, let him leave; the brother or the sister is not under bondage in such cases, but God has called us to peace." In the Greek the word for "not under bondage" is the same word as for slave (*dulos*). A slave is one who has absolutely no choice about the relationship.

When Paul used this word *dulos,* people of his day immediately knew what it meant — a slave who didn't have any vote, choice, or option. Paul says you are not a slave to the situation, because you do have an option to get out of that marriage.

Similarly, 1 Corinthians 7:39 says, "A wife is bound as long as her husband lives." But when the husband dies the wife is no longer bound. Wives are not slaves to that type of situation.

Let me caution you here. We have thus far discovered three justified reasons for divorce and remarriage: adultery, desertion, and sins (a bad marriage) committed prior to a salvation experience Now our tendency is to start rationalizing. You can tell you are rationalizing when you begin to think of a way out of your marriage instead of a way through your marriage. That's dangerous.

At times we begin to push in a direction that is ahead of God's Word or God's spirit for our lives. My feeling is that where God permits divorce and remarriage, we should accept it without fear or guilt. Let's not call "unclean" what He now calls clean. Neither should we try to put words in His mouth and make Him say what He, in fact, has not said (no matter how miserable we may be). There is something much worse than living with a mate in disharmony. It is living in disobedience to God. Let us be careful to have biblical grounds for what we do.

WHEN IS REMARRIAGE NOT ADVISABLE?

We've discovered there are certain times when it is permissible to remarry. We will now discover that even though you may have a right to remarry, it may not necessarily be right for you.

It's wrong for you to marry someone new if you have not yet overcome the problems which led to your previous marriage's dissolution. You should be asking yourself questions like: What caused the divorce? Has my former partner been remarried? Have I repented if the divorce was my fault? Have I sought solid Christian counseling? Have I tried to put the marriage to my former partner back together? It is important to confront these things and deal with them.

Consider 2 Corinthians 7:11. Paul gives us the finest verse concerning repentance in the Bible: "For behold what earnestness this very thing, this godly sorrow, has produced in you: what vindication of yourselves, what indignation, what fear, what longing, what zeal, what avenging of wrong!" The next statement is penetrating: "In everything you demonstrated yourselves to be innocent in the matter."

Paul, in effect, was saying, "I've looked at your life and I've seen that you have truly repented. You have gone the second mile, done everything you could to hold this together. You have demonstrated godly sorrow and repentance." Paul placed no blame on such a person.

Now, we all know that remarriages have worse odds of being successful than first marriages. The reason is that many of the past problems have not been resolved. Therefore, we carry our problems from our last marriage into our new marriage. We go along for a few months just fine, and then all of a sudden we're back in the same rut. We compare our new mate with our last mate. The same cycle occurs again because we never resolved our past problems. Things need to be in order. We cannot be in harmony with God if we lack harmony with our mates. We need to handle first things first.

A MATTER OF CONSCIENCE

If you don't have a conscience that is clear, don't remarry. If you have doubts about your new marriage, don't enter into it. Many times your best friends will press you to get married again. They'll say you need to get another mate. They'll say it's for your own good. They will try to play cupid. In Romans 14:23 we read, "But he who doubts is condemned if he eats, because

his eating is not from faith; and whatever is not from faith is sin."
This doesn't mean doubts that you have over common things.
There are concerns where we fear the same thing may happen to
us again. "Do I have the ability to make this mate happy? Am I
going to cause this marriage to blow up?" Even we who have
never been divorced have honest doubts when we enter our first
marriage. "Are we going to be happy? Is this for real? Is this
good? Am I truly in love?" These are simply pre-nuptial jitters.

But there can be more serious doubts. "Is remarriage really
right for me? Is this right? Is this going to help my relationship
with the Lord?" A divorced person should not be eager to remarry
until the circumstances with the former spouse show that all hope
of reconciliation is gone. One needs to make sure that the last
marriage is dead and cannot be resurrected.

It is wrong for you to marry if you left your last spouse because
you had your eye on someone else and were already committing
adultery (whether mentally or physically). It's wrong to remarry
in any situation in that case. In Mark 10:11-12, Jesus said, "Whoever
divorces his wife and remarries another woman commits adultery
against her; and if she herself divorces her husband and marries
another man, she is committing adultery." Jesus' references to
divorce and remarriage come in the very same sentence here. He
does not separate them in this passage. He says that if a man
divorces his wife in order to marry another woman, it is wrong
in the sight of God.

REMARRYING YOUR DIVORCED SPOUSE

As Christians, we have to understand that grace makes all things
possible. When people come to me and they say something just
can't be done, that the barrier is too high, I tell them to give
grace a chance. Grace can make the difference. But even with
grace, some barriers make remarriage to your former spouse either
difficult or impossible. For example, if the person you divorced
has already remarried, I do not advocate that you go and break
up that marriage to get your former spouse back. I do not think
two wrongs can make a right.

In Deuteronomy 24:1-4 God speaks to this very issue. He says
that if you have divorced your spouse and he or she has remarried,
you shouldn't try to get back together. I consider this option of
going back to your ex-mate closed when your former wife or

husband has remarried after your divorce.

Another barrier that would prevent you from going back to that marriage would be psychological and emotional barriers. It won't be good if every time you see that person, red flags begin to wave and bulls begin to run. You won't be able to see the possibility of new commitment, because all you will see will be problems. Sometimes, totally different lifestyles make marriage impossible to reunite.

Some Christians ask me if it is permissible for a Christian to remarry if the person he or she wants to marry is not a believer. I go back to the unequally yoked principle. If one has been divorced and wants to remarry, it is wrong to marry an unbeliever if one potential mate is a born-again Christian.

In 1 Corinthians 7:39 we see that if you are a widow, if your husband has died, you are not bound to him: ". . .but if her husband is dead, she is free to be married to whom she wishes, *only in the Lord.*" You are free to remarry, but only if you marry "in the Lord." That is the equally yoked principle.

As a Christian, you have no business dating a non-Christian. Absolutely none. God is not pleased with it. You can't rationalize it. He doesn't want you do to it. I know people will say, "I was not a Christian, and my wife was, and she dated me. We were married, and then I became a Christian." Just because a principle is violated and things come out right does not make the principle wrong. The principle is still right. As a believer you are not to get close to unbelievers. If you do, you're going to get one of those "wonderful" unbelievers under a full moon, and you're going to get in trouble. Then you'll come into the pastor's office with stars in your eyes. You'll say, "Now I know this probably should not have happened, but you can't believe how God worked this out." Don't bring God into the picture. God and the pastor don't want to be there with you. By the time you get stars in your eyes and you get to us, it's too late. God could have thunder and lightning crash in heaven and He could drop the commandment from the sky, "Thou shalt not marry him or her," but it wouldn't make any difference. You already would have had too many moons and violins and cruises on the bay. The only thing left for you to do is write a new theology book on why you should be allowed to run around with an unsaved person and be allowed to plan a marriage.

You may say that you have concern in your heart that your

espoused should be saved. Drop him or her like a hot potato and try your prayer life out. If you've got a good prayer life and he gets saved, go get him. Otherwise, steer clear.

TRYING TO COVER SIN

Look at 1 John 1:5-10. Though they don't want to admit it, in most cases of divorce both mates have had sin in their lives. I certainly believe there is the possibility of an innocent party. But *usually*, just as it takes two to make a good marriage, it takes two to make a bad one. Usually both mates have some sin that needs to be repented of. The remedy for sin and the criterion for fellowship is not sinlessness. It is an open acknowledgement of our sins and an appeal to God for forgiveness. When you read 1 John, you see that the whole thesis is that unconfessed sin, unrepentant sin, unacknowledged sin in the believer's life is the quickest way to lose good fellowship with God.

As we walk in obedience to the light that God gives us, we need to say to God, "I'm sorry; I was wrong. I grew angry with my wife. I should have been more forgiving. I wasn't, though." As we begin to admit things we not only get into right fellowship with God, but we also walk into a right relationship with our spouses.

WHAT CAN WE DO?

Understanding the issue of divorce and remarriage should not begin with what society says but with what God's Word says. My main responsibility as a pastor is to take the Word of God and study it. It's the pastor's responsibility to dig and learn. The greatest wrong a pastor does to his people is to come to the pulpit on Sunday with absolutely nothing to say. When you go to church, you ought to have your Bibles open and be ready to take notes. The pastor ought to be able to feed you truth from the Word of God, verse upon verse, so that you can see what God says. The pastor dishes it out, and you take it in. I don't mean you take notes and then file them away. If the Word of God is taught well, not only will you take those notes but there also will be change in your soul.

The church should model good Christian marriages in the leadership of the congregation. We've all read the little quote, "The best thing a father can do for his child is to love his mother." I'll tell you, the best thing the church can do is to put leaders in positions within the church whose marriages are solid. If a church leader's marriage is in trouble, he needs to leave his church responsibility and take care of his marriage.

I want you to understand that there are two levels of responsibility in the church. There is what I call the Christian membership level. That's the commitment you make to your church to be faithful and to support it with your finances and your time an your ministry. That's a level we ask every born-again believer who joins this church to commit himself to. But there is another level. The higher level is Christian leadership. The apostle Paul talks about this in his letters. He says there is one level for the Christian to live on, and he ought to keep growing. But there is a higher level on which the leaders of the church ought to live.

As a pastor, if my marriage is not together under God, so that it can be an example to my flock, I need to leave my position and take care of my marriage. My first responsibility is not to the congregation; my first responsibility is to my family. The best preaching I can do in my life is when I love my wife and kids and put them in the number one place. I love compliments and encouragement from members of my congregation, but the best thing I can hear is my wife Margaret saying to me, "Honey, that was a wonderful message." That's a 10. Regretfully, in the church world we've got a lot of problems in this area. I think the leaders of the church ought to have marriages that serve as examples to the flock.

The church should provide counseling and marriage seminars. It's the church's responsibility to provide wisdom and guidance. If you have a good marriage, you must keep working at it. If it is a poor one, you should seek Christian help and guidance. The main difference between the divorced couple and the nondivorced couple is not the size of their problems, but their mind-set in handling those problems. Many people who get divorced have fewer problems than other couples who stay together. But they do not have the willingness to work out their problems.

DISCIPLINE

It's the church's responsibility to discipline with love. In Galatians 6:1, we are taught that if a brother is caught in any trespass, the one who is spiritual is to restore such a one in the spirit of gentleness, each looking to himself lest he also become tempted. When two members of a church body have marriage problems, we must love and counsel them. If they are unscriptural in their divorce then we must discipline them, and show them where they are erring.

The church is responsible to keep members in and not cast them out. That is a general statement but what I mean is that when a marriage is on the rocks, we as a church, need to do our best to minister to both spouses and keep them both close to the church. We're not going to win by telling people where they're wrong and then kicking them out. If they are in leadership positions, they need to be removed from that responsibility. But basically, we should strive to minister to them. The church walks a fine line — the credibility of the church demands discipline, but the uniqueness of the church demands forgiveness. The purpose of discipline is not to kick someone out of the church. The purpose is to confront with the truth, encourage people, help them keep the truth, and bring them through that process to spiritual restoration and forgiveness.

As we noted earlier, in divorces there usually is no such thing as a totally innocent party. If it is your divorce, don't be on the defense. Just admit your shortcomings and talk to God about them. Don't run and hide. This is natural for us. The first reaction when there is a problem of this nature is to run away from the church because, truthfully, the church has not always been as loving as it should be. Sometimes your conscience bothers you. But remember, God's people are *your* people.

Don't exact the law on your mate. The law will separate you. Grace will heal you. If you judge with the law, you will be judged by the law. If you show grace, grace will be shown to you.

Follow the Word, not the world. The Bible is your guide for marital matters. The world asks the question, "Are you being treated fairly?" The Word asks, "Are you exercising forgiveness?" **The world says, "You don't have to take that." The Word says, "Walk the second mile and turn the other cheek." The world says, "Everyone else is getting a divorce." The Word says, "Broad is the way that leads to destruction and many will go therein." The world says, "Think of yourself." The Word says, "Think of others." The world says, "There is nothing you can do." The Word says, "I can do all things through Christ who strengthens me." There's a lot of difference. Let's sum it up.**

SUMMARY

Divorce is not God's will. It may happen, but it's not God's ideal nor His standard.

With the curse of sin came the potential for divorce. That's where it happened. It all started back in the garden of Eden.

God permits divorce on the grounds of adultery or desertion by an unbeliever. That's from a Christian perspective. Those are the two areas where He permits it.

The standard of Christian marriages is higher than the standard for non-Christian marriages. But the assistance for Christian marriages is greater than the assistance for non-Christian marriages. As God's family, we have God's power, God's grace, Christian friends, all kinds of assistance and help that should enable us to love better and have better marriages.

Usually, there is not a totally innocent party. Therefore, admittance and confession of sin is essential. The more obvious offense does not necessarily mean the greater sin.

A believer is never to marry an unbeliever. Christians are to be equally yoked.

Divorce is not the unpardonable sin. Therefore, there is forgiveness.

There is something much worse than living with a mate in disharmony. It is living with God in disobedience.

A Christian should search for a way *through* instead of a way *out* of the marriage.

The leaders of the church must set good examples for Christian marriages. They must be models of what God intended.

The attitude of the church toward divorce must reflect the attitude of Jesus. The attitude of Jesus was, "Neither do I condemn thee, go and sin no more." That should be our attitude, too.

CHAPTER 8

How Can
I Deal With
the Guilt I Feel?

Few human emotions are as disturbing and painful as feelings of guilt and failure. Since the voice of the conscience speaks from inside the human mind, we cannot escape its unrelenting reminders of our mistakes and sins. Probably, of all the emotions, guilt hangs on heaviest.

There are several types of guilt. For example, there is guilt before God. This is when we violate God's laws — the scriptural, ethical, moral teachings of God's word.

There is also guilt before man. That is when we violate the social ethics of a particular culture. There is a difference between the laws of God and the laws of man. God's laws never change; they always are the same. They have a continuity from the very beginning. We operate under His laws today just as people did 3,000 years ago. However, in man's laws, rules vary from culture to culture, from country to country, and from century to century. If you're in America and drive a car, you drive on the right side of the road. If you're in England, you drive on the left side. Man's laws are temporary, circumstantial, and regional. God's laws are steadfast and timeless.

Within man's laws we can develop a social guilt. That's when I am guilty of doing something that is not socially acceptable. If you asked me to come to your home for an evening and we enjoyed a lovely meal, and I did not say thank you or show my gratitude, I would be violating that law.

There is also such a thing as false guilt, that is, feelings of guilt when no actual wrong has been done to anyone. This guilt usually stems from rejection in childhood. It is imposed upon us, and it literally tears us apart. There's a vast difference between real guilt and false guilt. I want you to understand the difference from a Christian perspective, so you will know when to repent. Perhaps you are repenting over things that don't need repentance. Perhaps you are living with things that need to be buried.

True guilt is a feeling generated by divine judgment. It's when God speaks to us after we have broken one of His divine laws. False guilt results from the judgment of men. There's a lot of difference. We have true guilt when we have broken God's standards of life. False guilt is when we are told that we have broken some person's standard for our life. We begin to try to please that person, and we come under bondage.

Furthermore, true guilt is constructive because it results in repentant sorrow. When I speak of repentant sorrow, I'm talking about that positive change of behavior that makes us better people, better Christians. It is a convicting feeling, a sense of deep need to change. It becomes a compulsion within us.

False guilt is psychological guilt. Confusion reigns in psychological guilt. If you are burdened with guilt and you cannot pinpoint why you have such feelings, it is probably false guilt. "I just feel guilty," is a common statement among people who have false guilt. When God is dealing with you about guilt, there needs to be repentance and the blood of Jesus applied. He will always be clear in dealing with that guilt.

Constructive sorrow produces a positive change of behavior. Conviction simply means that God is clearly showing us our sins and admonishing us to change. In other words, if we really do something wrong, God lets us know — not by guilt or fear of punishment, but by conviction and a call to turn from sin. We then ask forgiveness and make the necessary changes in our lives. Nowhere in the Bible does God tell us to punish ourselves over and over again with guilt and remorse for our past sins.

True guilt is when the Holy Spirit uses our conscience to tell us we have sinned. False guilt is when we feel burdened and worthless. Our self-worth is attacked. Our conscience nurtures guilt feelings and blows them out of proportion. False guilt would be like Job's friends who came and said, "You surely have sinned." They were trying to lay false guilt upon one of God's servants.

Someone asked a six-year-old boy what he thought a conscience was. He said, "It's that thing that makes me feel bad when I kick little girls." Now you may not be going around kicking little girls, but conscience is that thing that makes you feel bad sometimes. Each person's conscience varies. Some people have a tender conscience. They are like violets; they are easily crushed. Then there are are those who are like a tulips; their conscience blooms for awhile and then goes away. It blooms again and goes away. Some are like wild roses; nothing affects them. They're just tough and seem to be totally unaware of right and wrong and what God is trying to say to them.

All of us have had an experience similar to that of Willie in the comic strip, MOON MULLINS. He is slumped in a chair in front of a TV set, coffee cup resting on his pot belly. As he flicks his cigar ashes in his coffee cup, he says, "You're awful quiet this morning, Mamie."

"I've decided to let your conscience be your guide on your day off, Willie," Mamie replies.

In the next picture Willie is outside surrounded by a lawnmower, a rake and a hoe, and is frantically washing the windows. "Every time I listen to that darn thing," he mutters, "I end up ruinin' my relaxin'!"

We all can identify with what he is saying. Our conscience has the ability to come into our lives at any time and talk to us. That can be good. From a Christian perspective there are several biblical functions of a conscience. In the Latin word for "conscience" the prefix means "with" or "together." The latter part of that word means "to know." In the Greek it means "to agree with." In the Latin it means "to know together." So, in a Christian perspective, conscience means to know and agree with God. You are walking in the light as He is in the light. You are having fellowship with Him. That relationship is clear; it is the way it should be. An 18th century philosopher said, "Two things fill my mind with ever increasing wonders and awe. . .the starry heavens above me and the moral law within me."

From a biblical perspective the conscience does three things:

(1) *The conscience bears witness to us.* Romans 9:1 says, "I am telling the truth in Christ, I am not lying, my conscience bearing me witness in the Holy Spirit." The words, "bearing me witness," are in the present tense. Paul is saying my conscience continually bears witness unto me of what I am saying.

(2) *The conscience accuses or excuses us.* In Romans 2:15, Paul said the thoughts of the unbelievers were alternately accusing and defending them. The conscience can be our accuser or our excuser.

(3) *The conscience judges our actions.* In 2 Corinthians 1:12, Paul says, "For our proud confidence is this." He is saying, "My confidence is in the testimony of my conscience; that is, holiness and godly sincerity. My pride is in clear conscience," It judges us. Now, there are characteristics about the conscience: It's clear, unbiased and individualistic.

The conscience receives the information given to it and pronounces a verdict on it. Very seldom do you run into someone who says, "I *think* my conscience is bothering me." It is either bothering him or it's not. He may not know the issue, but he knows his conscience is bothering him. It may not always be right, but it is clear. It gives its judgments but supplies no reason. It does not say why it judges an action in a particular way, but says only that the action is right or wrong. It is unbiased and strict.

One's conscience is uniquely based on a person's teachings and experiences. Thus, one person's conscience is different from another's. What offends one will not offend another. Many times it's just because of environment. But we need to see that the conscience is not infallible. We hear the expression, "Let your conscience be your guide." It can be bad advice. The conscience is the vehicle that God gives us to help us live right. But, if you feed into the conscience wrong information, it will give out bad signals.

We can't know for sure, of course, but there is no evidence that Adolph Hitler experienced any serious measure of self-condemnation toward the end of his life, despite the torment he had inflicted on the world. How could he cope with the knowledge that, at his order, millions of innocent Jewish children were torn from the arms of their screaming parents and thrown into gas chambers or shot by SS troops? In 1944, when the Allied armies were closing in on Germany, thousands of naked children and babies were exposed to snowstorms and doused with water to cause their deaths by freezing. Hitler conceived and implemented this horrible "final solution," but he is never known to have uttered a word of self-doubt or remorse.

Likewise, Joseph Stalin is said to have murdered between 20 and 30 million people during his long dictatorship; yet, his conscience apparently remained quiet and unprovoked to the end. There was no obvious deathbed repentance or regret. He simply asked his wife to read him some short stories by Jack London, which she did, and then Stalin went peacefully into the arms of Death. My point is that the voice of disapproval from within is a fragile thing in some people. It can be seared and ignored until its whisper of protest is no longer heard. Perhaps the most effective silencer from the conscience is found in widespread social opinions. If everybody is doing it — the reasoning goes — it can't be very harmful or sinful.

One study reveals that 66 percent of today's college students feel it is O.K. (i.e, not guilt producing) to have sexual intercourse with someone they have dated and "like a lot." One quarter of all individuals of college age have shared a bedroom with a member of the opposite sex for three months or more.

You see, if these same "liberated" young people had participated in that kind of sexual behavior twenty years ago, most of them would have had to deal with feelings of guilt and remorse. Now, however, they are lulled into a false sense of security by the fact that their behavior is socially acceptable. Individual guilt is partially a product of collective attitudes and concepts of morality, despite the fact that God's standards are eternal and are not open to revision or negotiation. His laws will remain in force even if the whole world rejects them, as in the days of Noah.

I am saying that the conscience is an imperfect mental faculty. There are times when it condemns us for mistakes and human frailties that can't be avoided; at other times it will remain silent in the face of indescribable wickedness.

Now on the flip side, it's possible to feel guilt and be innocent. It's possible for me to have guilt feelings, and yet in God's eyes be perfectly redeemed.

Note 2 Corinthians 11:4. That's where Paul indicates that Satan presents himself as an angel of light. In other words, he's a false representative of God. Undeserved guilt is one of Satan's ways of plaguing God's people. He uses discouragement to burden and weigh down believers. He causes them to be reminded of former sins and to worry about them even though God has forgiven the believers for these past wrongs. What better tool to foster discouragement than to create feelings of guilt?

THE CONSCIENCE AT WORK

Matthew 26 tells the story of Jesus eating His last meal with the disciples before His death. It was a time of intimacy. In that passage Jesus looked at those who belonged to Him and talked to them about falling away. When He began to talk about their falling away Peter spoke up and said something like, "I can't speak for the rest of these men, but I'm telling You, You can count on me." He wanted Jesus to know he would be faithful. The Lord looked at him and said, "Before the rooster crows in the morning, you'll deny Me three times." Now here is the theme and the thesis of this entire chapter: God's love is a rooster that crows.

Most of us have had experiences with roosters and chickens. I can remember as a four-year-old boy going out to a farm with a member of my dad's church. While there, a rooster came up who thought I was infringing on his territory. I'll never forget how he pecked me on the leg. That produced within me the ability to run very fast. I turned and ran like crazy with that rooster right on my heels.

That rooster's name was Big Stuff. And he was. Big Stuff was his name and the barnyard was his domain. I withdrew from his domain very rapidly. My mother saw me coming and got the barnyard gate opened so I could get out of the way of Big Stuff.

In perspective to guilt, I'm saying God allows a rooster to come into the life of a Christian periodically to crow, to tell us we're off base. The rooster tells us we're not what we could be or ought to be. It happened in Peter's life. Two thousand years ago a rooster crowed. There were two men, followers of Jesus, one named Peter who listened to the rooster and he lived; another was Judas, who didn't and died. The crowing rooster is an appropriate symbol of an early warning system God has graciously built into each of us. It's called a conscience.

You say, "Pastor, why do roosters crow in my life?" Well, first of all, because you don't heed the warnings of the Scripture. In Matthew 26:31, Jesus taught the apostles that they would be scattered and would fall away. In verses 33-35 He tells Peter he would deny Him. Peter insisted he would not. In verse 41, in the garden, Jesus said to keep watching and praying so that they would not enter into temptation. The spirit was willing but the flesh was weak. More than once, Jesus told them to be careful — to watch out! Because Peter didn't listen to the warnings of the Scripture, he grew troubled and God brought a rooster to crow.

Secondly, God places a rooster in our lives at times when we think we are stronger spiritually than we truly are. Can't you just hear Peter saying he would never deny Jesus? You see, when the fires of temptation and trials are burning hot, resolutions and commitments and good intentions are prone to go up in smoke. That's why Paul says in 1 Corinthians 10:12 to be careful if you think you are standing because you might fall. Take heed. Don't get too self-assured in this relationship. I would like to think I can do it on my own. But just about the time I think I can, God brings a rooster into my life. The rooster crows and it reminds me that I am not strong enough in myself.

Finally, God brings a rooster into our lives to admonish us about yielding to peer pressure. That's what happened to Peter. He was hoping to blend in with the crowd. He was hoping to be one of the boys. He went into the courtyard and a servant identified him as one of the disciples. He said, "No!" He went out by the gate and somebody confronted him. "No!" The third person came up. We know the story. The fact is this: There are times when you and I get sucked into things because of our friends or colleagues. Maybe it's at the job. Our good resolutions and the things we want to do for God all of a sudden begin to be washed away. They become neutralized by the conflicting expectations of other people. When that happens God allows a rooster to crow in our lives.

If your heart is to please God, as Peter's was, God won't let you go too far without allowing a rooster to cross your path and crow. As soon as Peter began to curse and swear and say he did not know Jesus, *immediately* the cock crowed. You see, God is never going to let you fall into sin and wake up someday and say "He didn't warn me." I run into people all the time who say, "I don't know how I got so messed up." Yes, you do. God put a rooster in your life and it began to crow and you knew you were disobeying God, but you kept on doing it. You did not pay attention.

Two men heard the rooster crow that morning. Judas died and Peter lived. How should we respond if a rooster crows in our lives? What shall we do? We're talking about guilt and conscience. There are five things that Peter did, and I want to encourage you to do the same.

1. He Remembered the Word of the Lord

"And immediately the cock crowed and Peter remembered the Word that Jesus said." How beautiful it is when we hear the rooster crow in our spiritual walk with God and we remember the Word of God. We go back to that which is steadfast and sure and clear. David said that when he was disobedient and didn't heed the rooster crowing in his life, he was drained physically and emotionally and was messed up spiritually.

So, when the rooster crows in your life, the first thing to do is go back to the Word of God and find out what it has to say to you.

2. He Removed Himself From the Place of Temptation

When the rooster crowed he thought, *Hey! Wait a minute! I'm getting out of here.* Look at Matthew 26:75: "He went out." Peter had denied the Lord. He realized he was obviously not able to handle the pressure around him. He did what each one of us should do when we sense the rooster is crowing. We ought to look at our associates, our surroundings, and find out how much they are affecting us and our spiritual walk with God.

3. He Repented

Look at verse 75. When Peter went out, he "wept bitterly." He was heartbroken, crushed, shamed, guilt-ridden. He had done the impossible, the horrible. He had sold out his faith. He had sold out his calling, his best friend. When Peter heard that rooster crow, Luke tells us that he saw Jesus and Jesus saw him. Undoubtedly there was hurt written all over the face of our Lord. Peter, why did you do it?

Peter wept tears of bitterness. But it wasn't a bitterness at Jesus, the Romans, the economy, the world situation, or the fisherman's retirement fund. Peter was bitter at himself for not listening, for always pushing, for being so arrogant, so sure, so shallow, so unstable, so weak, so rotten, so wretched. His hopes, his dreams, his idealism, his future rode his tears into the dust. He felt it was over. He felt finished. Judas committed suicide. Certainly that idea must have occurred to Peter, too.

Peter's tears could not be labeled "tears of remorse." Regret?

Perhaps. But primarily Peter shed tears of repentance. Could Jesus forgive? Could He cleanse, could He forget, could He welcome him again as a friend? Tears of repentance water the future with hope. They are sweet, life-giving. Tears of remorse, by contrast, are usually hot and bitter, filled with anger and resentment.

A fork in the road confronts the wayward Christian when the rooster crows. He ultimately must choose between the path of repentance and the path of remorse. *Remorseful* people are upset because they got caught and are facing judgment, punishment or censure. *Repentant* people are grieved because they failed someone who loves them.

4. Peter Reaffirmed His Love for Jesus

In John 21 after the resurrection of our Lord, Jesus said, "Peter, do you love Me?" "Yes, I love You," Peter answered, and he meant it. Jesus had forgiven Peter for his lapse of loyalty and had absolved Peter of his feelings of guilt. Once more they were friends.

5. Jesus Recommissioned Peter for Ministry

Jesus looked into the eyes of Peter and said, "You messed up, but Peter, you listened to the rooster when it crowed. I'm going to use you for My glory."

I had someone ask me one time, "What would Jesus have done with Judas if he would not have hung himself? What if Judas, when he heard the cock crow, had repented like Peter?" He would have forgiven Judas and used him just as He used Peter. Absolutely. That's grace. Grace forgives and covers all our sin.

If the rooster crows in your life, deal directly with your sin. Get it behind you.

You *can* stand guiltless before Christ.

CHAPTER 9

What Is the Best Way to Share My Faith?

In John, chapter 4, Jesus talked to a lady about eternal life. You can share your faith effectively with friends, too. Most of you know someone who needs to know Christ as Savior. If I can share with you how to be a witness and you use that knowledge to share your faith with some friends, and they receive Christ, the kingdom of God will be multiplied.

When we talk about sharing faith, witnessing and winning souls, most folks develop fear. They are afraid they won't know what to say. Some people feel they have to have a doctorate in theology before they can witness to someone.

Let me tell you about Steve. He was one of the most reserved people I have ever met. He was the kind of guy who, if you asked him a question, would give you a one-word answer.

"How are you doing today, Steve?"

"Fine."

"How's your family?"

"Fine."

"How's your work coming along?"

"Fine."

"Did you enjoy the services today?"

"Yes." One word.

Now, Steve had a wife named Georgia. She made up for him in talking. Georgia had the gift of interpretation. I have seen her interpret his one-word answers for him. They were a beautiful couple. One month I decided I would teach evangelism. I never will forget walking out and seeing right in front of me quiet, shy, timid, one-word Steve. I'll be honest, I looked at him and I thought, *what is he doing here?* I was going to talk about sharing one's faith, and anybody knows it takes more than one word to do that. You just don't walk up to somebody and say, "Saved?" and then wait for a moment and ask, "Yes?" "No?"

Well, I taught the series of lessons, and Steve was there every time. Finally we came to a place where I had taught them enough that I could ask, "Do you have any questions?"

Steve raised his hand, and I got excited because he was going to ask a question and that meant he was finally going to say more than one word! He said, "Pastor, I don't know if you've noticed since you've come to this church or not, but I'm kind of quiet and shy." Fooled me, Steve, fooled me. He said, "I really don't talk a lot, and I have a friend that I ride to work with every day that I would love to lead to Jesus. What can I do?"

I had prayer with Steve that night. Afterward, he said he was going to lead his friend to Christ the next day.

The rest of this story I learned from Georgia. She said, "Steve came home that night, and he was scared to death. I mean he was frightened! This was white-knuckle time!" She said he opened his Bible, took out his pen, and started to mark the Scriptures I had given him in class. Then he went to bed and tossed and turned for about 15 minutes. Then he got up and marked more Scriptures. All night he did that, down and up, down and up. He was a nervous wreck. Finally, about 5:30 he picked up his lunch box and his Bible and headed off to Western Electric in Columbus, Ohio, about thirty miles away.

He went across to the east side of Lancaster. His friend, Jack, got in the car. Steve said, "Good morning, Jack."

Jack said, "Good morning, Steve."

Steve said, "Jack, you need to be a Christian. And I've got to drive to work today so here's the Bible." Steve gave him the Bible and said, "I marked the verses and you start with number one where the marker is. I'm going to drive to work, and I want you to read the Bible and get saved."

Steve grabbed hold of the steering wheel, never looked to his right for thirty miles, scared to death, and drove. Finally after thirty minutes he had to look at his friend. He was nervous; his hands were sweaty on that wheel. He took a big gulp and looked to his right. Jack had the Bible opened on his lap with tears flowing down his cheeks. Steve looked at his friend and said, "Jack, would you like me to pray with you?"

Jack said, "Yes," They pulled into the parking lot of Western Electric that day, and Jack became a believer in the Lord Jesus Christ.

I tell that story for this reason. Many people do not share their faith with others because they do not feel adequate. They feel like Steve. I run into people all the time who say, "Pastor, you've got to understand that that's just not my gift. I am just not cut out for evangelism." Some tell me, "I'm the quiet type, the shy type, I just don't like to meet new people." I would be the first to grant you, as a pastor and also a Bible teacher, that there are some people who have the gift, and are much more effective soul-winners than others. We are all different. That's good. Yet, Jesus said we are all to be witnesses. He didn't say in the Great Commission that you who have the desire to evangelize are to be witnesses and the rest of you are to take it easy. He said we are all to be witnesses.

My responsibility as a pastor is to equip people to be effective witnesses. How can you effectively share your faith? We all acknowledge we have unsaved friends and family members. What I want to do is use Jesus as the model, and John chapter 4, to help us learn how to share our faith effectively with others. In John 4:1-54 Jesus is at a well in Samaria, and He is about to share eternal life with a lady who has come to get some water from the well.

The first thing I see unfolded in this great model of sharing our faith is that Jesus did not allow His feelings to affect His witnessing. Look with me at verse 6: Jesus was at Jacob's well, and "being wearied from His journey, was sitting thus by the well." Now the words that stand out to me in verse 6 are the words "being wearied from His journey." You see, Jesus was worn out, tired. He had just finished some full days of ministry and the last thing, I think, Jesus wanted to do then was preach or teach again. I think He wanted to rest. I think He wanted a drink of water.

The disciples had gone to town to buy some food. Jesus physically was not strong enough to go with them. He sat by the well, waiting for the disciples to bring back the food. Notice that

Jesus did not allow his weariness or feelings to affect His witnessing. I want you to understand this: For years the church has taught that we have to have some unbelievably large burden for lost people before we can ever become effective in witnessing. That is not true. In fact, what is more true is this: You come into a service or a large missions rally where you see the potential of the harvest and there is a sense of stirring emotionally. That's good. But it is also true that when you leave the sanctuary and go to a restaurant, or go home, prepare dinner and change your clothes, by about 2 in the afternoon that overwhelming emotional feeling to win the world for Jesus Christ has certainly escaped you.

As a pastor and church leader, I learned long ago that the best way to teach people the art of sharing faith and winning others was to teach them that they don't do it by burden. You don't do it because you feel like it. If you wait until you feel like it, you will never do it. We see our neighbor across the fence and know we should share our faith, and I guarantee nine times out of ten you won't feel like doing it. This may surprise you, but sometimes at 5 on Sunday morning I do not feel like preaching. I don't have some of my highest spiritual moments at that time. When you begin to share your faith with somebody, and you're not sure how they will react to you, I guarantee that you are not going to feel super about it. There are going to be times when you say, "Oh, I hope I don't have to share my faith." Don't become a spiritual pygmy because you don't always *feel* like witnessing. It's true that the world is run by tired men and it's true that the kingdom of God is built by tired men.

I will venture to say this: If you are a Christian and you consistently share your faith with others, it won't take long for you to realize that you should share Christ with others, *not* because you *feel* like it, but because it is *right*. Nothing more, nothing less. I'm sorry to take all the pizzazz out of this chapter. But if I can develop a dozen or fifteen people, today, who will just be people of pure character, operating their Christian life on the principles of what is right (not on what they feel like doing), we will begin to develop strong disciples in the area of sharing their faith. So, do what is right, not what you "feel" like doing.

MEETING PEOPLE ON THEIR LEVELS

When the Lord began to talk to the woman at the well about

the areas with which she was familiar, they had commonality — water — in their conversation. He began to talk to her on her level of understanding. It is very important to meet people on a level to which they can relate. I would encourage you to buy a book called *Out of the Saltshaker* by Rebecca Pippert. I probably have read a hundred books on evangelism, but Rebecca does a better job than anyone else I've ever read. She explains how to live the lifestyle of evangelism, which is neither forced nor legalistic. Jesus said we are the salt of the earth, and Rebecca tells us to get out of the saltshaker and touch our world.

I want to quote a few sentences from that book. On page 24 she writes, "Our problem in evangelism is not that we don't have enough information. It is that we don't know how to be ourselves. We forget that we are called to be witnesses to what we have seen and know, not to what we don't know. The key is authenticity and obedience, not a doctorate in theology."

Isn't that good? She's saying, "Hey, you can be just like Steve. You don't have to know the difference between premillenialism and postmillenialism. You don't have to explain transubstantiation. You don't have to expound on antinomianism. You don't have to know about the Hittites, Jebusites, and Amorites. No, no."

Rebecca tells us that if we have received Christ, have been brought out of darkness into light and out of spiritual death into spiritual life, we are witnesses to what has happened to us. All we have to do is be ourselves.

You don't have to get a Bible like your pastor's, take it under your arm and go knocking door to door. Just relax, let Jesus shine from your life.

The personal need the Lord had in John 4 was a need for water. The Bible says, "There came a woman of Samaria to draw water. Jesus said to her, 'Give me a drink.'"

The thing I want us to understand is that we never win people to Christ by acting as if we have all the answers. Let's face it — is there anything more disgusting in life than to run into somebody who thinks he has all the answers? Doesn't someone like that just bug you to death?

But Jesus was casual and friendly. He asked the woman for a drink of water. He kept things simple, humble, and kind.

Have you ever asked anybody for directions? I don't care where you are or what culture it is, if you roll down the window and say, "Please help me find such-and-such a place," people will stop and give you directions. And if there are three or four of them in the conversation, if one can't help you, before you know it the other three volunteer advice. And I mean they really tell you how to get there, even draw maps for you. They will stop anything to help you out. Their last words are standards: "You can't miss it."

"Three blocks, turn to the right. Yes sir, go two lights and turn left. Go down the alley and make another left. Turn right there and go behind the garage and the parking lot. Make a U-turn, go over the bridge, and you can't miss it."

I always want to say, "You want to make a bet?" I could collect a lot of bets if I could find those folks again after I got lost. But people love to give directions and help out.

All the Lord did was to help this lady build her self-esteem by giving her an opportunity to help out. He didn't say, "Lady, sit down, have I got a message for you!" He said, instead, "You are important enough for me to start this conversation on a level you can easily relate to."

"The Samaritan woman therefore said to Him, 'How is it that You, being a Jew, ask me for a drink since I am a Samaritan woman?'" This lady was a Samaritan, and the Jews, the Bible tells us, had no dealings with Samaritans. Culturally and socially they were of different classes. But the Lord died for all. We Gentiles would have been outsiders, too, because He was Jewish. John 1:11-12 says, "He came to His own and His own received Him not. But as many as received Him, to them gave He power to become the Sons of God" (KJV). In other words, He died for everyone. He had the ability to look past barriers, questions, problems and prejudices.

SPIRITUAL CONVERSATIONS

In John 4:10 we are shown how Jesus accepted the water from the woman and then used it as a way of witnessing to her. "Jesus answered and said to her, 'If you knew the gift of God, and who it is who says to you 'Give Me a drink,' you would have asked Him and He would have given you living water.'" He had the ability to convert secular conversations to spiritual conversations.

It's easy to talk to our neighbors and friends and loved ones about vacation, work, the job. But have you ever asked yourself why it is so difficult for you to talk about the spiritual part of your life? I've known pastors who have gone into hospitals to talk about the physical, what kind of medicine patients are taking, what the doctor is saying, when they are going to get out of the hospital, and so on, but never about the spiritual. Jesus made a transference from the secular to the spiritual.

Rebecca Pippert says, "The closer we are in our walk with God, the easier it is to make that transference." I've asked God to give me wisdom in teaching this very important subject. It is extremely difficult for many of you to witness to your family and friends because for years you've not talked to them about spiritual things. Suddenly, for you now to introduce Christ into the conversation would be such a change, not only would you sense it, but your friend or loved one would, too.

When I committed myself to be a soul-winner, I made a commitment to the Lord. I don't want to put my commitments on you because I'm not Moses coming off the mountain with the Ten Commandments. But the following commitment has helped me: If I have time to talk to a person in a one-to-one conversation for fifteen minutes, then I'm going to share Christ with him or her. That doesn't mean I'm going to get out the Bible and preach, but that does mean that in that fifteen-minute period of time I'm going to let that person know in some wonderful, kind, and tactful way that I'm sold out to Jesus.

Because of that commitment I have seen hundreds of people come to Jesus Christ. I learned early in sharing my faith that the longer I waited, the longer I put off bringing Christ or spiritual things into the conversation, the more difficult it would be to talk about Jesus. Just try it. Sit down with somebody and get acquainted and talk for thirty minutes and think, *I could share Christ with them.* The longer you talk without doing it, the harder it will be to get Him into the picture.

It's very interesting. The Lord did not allow the Samaritan woman's lack of understanding in spiritual things to stop Him from sharing. It's obvious in verses 11 through 14 that she did not understand about living water. She asked how you can have water that will cause you not to thirst again. She was totally confused. But Jesus just lovingly kept sharing, explaining how to do it.

In John 4:14, Jesus talked about drinking water that quenches a thirst forever. He transferred the woman's physical need to her spiritual needs. He talked about water in order to gain her attention.

A few years ago I went to a hospital to visit a cousin of one of my church members. The cousin was not a Christian, and my member expressed the desire that I share Christ with him if the opportunity arose. In the same room was another man who informed me upon getting acquainted that he was a deacon in a church. We had a very warm conversation and I asked both of the men if they had the assurance they were going to heaven. The cousin immediately said, "No," but the other man looked at me and said, "Of course. I'm the deacon of a church." At the close of that comment, he picked up a newspaper and began to read. I then directed most of my attention to the cousin, who had expressed doubt about going to heaven.

As I began to share, however, I sensed this deacon was not a Christian and needed also to hear this message. Even though I was directing my eye contact to the doubtful man, I spoke loud enough for the deacon to hear me. "Let me tell you about Nicodemus, a religious man in the Bible who was a deacon in his church." My deacon friend heard me, put his newspaper down and listened to my conversation with the cousin of my church member. I explained that although Nicodemus was a faithful worker in God's church, he still lacked a personal relationship with the God of that church. I shared with them both how they could have the assurance of going to heaven through a relationship with Jesus Christ. God enabled me to do double witnessing that day.

Many times we need to ask God to give us special wisdom in sharing our faith. The more we practice sharing our faith, the more insight God gives us concerning the key that will unlock the doors to people's hearts. The old saying, "Practice makes perfect," is certainly applicable here.

In John 4:15-19, the woman at the well began to talk to Jesus, and the conversation came around to her serious marriage problems. In fact, she had gone through five husbands and was now living with a man who was not her husband. We see that the Lord had wisdom not to get side-tracked but, instead, to keep her focused where she needed to be — on the living water.

I used to read the verse, "He who winneth souls is wise." I used to look at that verse and say, "Wow! Does the Old Testament writer really mean that if you win souls you are wise?" Yes. In fact, I will explain that. When the Scriptures says, "He who winneth souls is wise," it means that a person who shares his faith meets all kinds of people with all kinds of situations with all kinds of different questions. That Christian who is witnessing learns to give answers to all types of problems. The end result is a wisdom that God's spirit gives the believer.

In fact, when I used to share my faith and folks would ask me a question I didn't know how to answer, I would say, "I don't know. But if you will allow me, I'll find it in the Scriptures and come back tomorrow and share the answer with you." After I did that a couple dozen times I had the answers. Now you can ask me questions and I can answer them quite readily. Why? Because I've done it so often. I have gained wisdom. James also tells us that if we lack wisdom we can ask it of God. There is nothing that makes us more dependent upon God than sharing our faith. It is an exciting challenge.

I remember my evangelism course in college. We used a thirteen-page book. What was great about that book was that it not only had the questions to ask an unsaved person, but it also had the answers. I thought this was wonderful. Someone was smart enough to write a book with both the questions and the answers. I thought all I had to do was memorize that book and then I could win the world.

As soon as I memorized the book, I went out to try it, and knocked on the door of a lady's house. I asked her the first question, and you can never in your life imagine what happened. That lady answered it wrong! She did. She missed the questions. I gulped and thought, *What do I do now!* I felt like running back to my 1964 Falcon parked outside her house, pulling out the book, waving it under her nose and asking, "Haven't you ever read this book?"

Well, I thought, *anyone can miss one question.* I boldly went to the second one. She missed that one, too. By this time I really didn't know what to do. I was 0 for 2. I remember backing off that porch, stumbling down the steps, and hurrying to my car. Evangelism was over for me. I pulled away from her house looking out of the corner of my left eye. I can still see that lady standing by her doorway with a great look of amazement on her face. She must have been thinking, *What was he trying to do?*

Right then I said what a whole bunch of you would say, "I just don't have *that* gift! I'm free. I don't have to do that anymore. That certainly isn't my strength." Do you know what Mark Twain said? "If a cat sits on a hot stove, that cat will never sit on a hot stove again. The problem is, it'll never sit on a cold stove either." I'm telling you, every time that cat sees a stove he is gone. That's how I felt about personal witnessing for a long time.

FOCUSING ON SALVATION

As Jesus talked to the Samaritan woman, He had to work to keep her mind on the topic of personal salvation. The woman interrupted with a story about how her father worshipped on a mountain. She threw questions at Jesus, particularly about where He went to church. Jesus explained to her that the issue at hand was not what church a person attended but, rather, whether or not a person had accepted Christ as Lord.

To help the woman comprehend His message, Jesus built upon the bit of religious knowledge the woman already had. The woman said, "I know that Messiah is coming. . .when that One comes, He will declare all things to us." Having thus led her that far in their conversation, Jesus revealed Himself to her by saying, "I who speak to you am He." He waited until her heart was ready and then He revealed Himself to her. She acknowledged Him as Lord and went away glad-hearted.

Interestingly enough, Jesus, too, was glad-hearted. When the apostles returned with food and supplies, Jesus told them He wasn't hungry. They asked why and He said, "I've already feasted." The woman's conversion had given Him vitality and energy.

Many times I have been tired when I began sharing Christ with another person. I always find myself refreshed at the end of the conversation. I am ready to share with another! Why? There is strength and nourishment in doing God's will.

Jesus said, ". . .lift up your eyes, and look on the fields, that they are white for harvest." You don't see the harvest field until you see a person. What you find when you share your faith with someone will raise your whole level of understanding and your desire to share with others. Vision always begins with one. When we are faithful over a few things, we become ruler over many.

How do you multiply God's kingdom? You start with one person. Don't start with the whole county. Start with a friend. Perhaps he or she already has expressed a hunger for spiritual things. Begin there. I wish I had space to write about my friend Jim whom I led to the Lord, who led Vic Rader to the Lord, who led Tom Ferrell to the Lord, who led Jim Vanover to the Lord, who led Mike Hines to the Lord, who led Jeff Smithto the Lord. You say, that's great, pastor, one who leads one, who leads another, who leads another. . . .Yes, five out of the six today either have entered into or are studying for the ministry. It started with just one.

The challenge is not, "Let's win all of our city to Jesus Christ." No. That's frustrating, probably impossible. Here's the challenge. Let's win one to Jesus Christ. Start where you are.

CHAPTER 10

Where Is God When Things Go Wrong?

Not long ago, I sat in a restaurant with a very high ranking police officer in our city. I listened to him for a few hours as he poured out his heart concerning the McDonald's restaurant tragedy of 1984 when a lone gunman went berserk and slaughtered everyone in sight. He told me stories that he could not share with his wife because she was having nightmares over the incident. I listened to him relate one story after another as he sought logical answers for such chaos.

While I was preparing a message recently, I received a call from two members of my church. Their grandson of two months had died of SIDS (crib death). How do you explain those things? How do you bring comforting answers to hurting hearts? I believe any pastor would tell you that we don't "punch in and punch out" when it come to our work schedule. We carry home the burdens of our congregation and wrestle with tough questions late into the night.

There is seldom a day that goes by in which just reading a newspaper won't make you wonder. "Is God really in control?" The headlines are depressing. "Plane Fires Rocket, Hits Tanker in Gulf," "U.S. Refuses to Aid Child With Lethal Skin Ailment," "Salvadoran Military Officials Unhappy With U.S. Military Advisors," etc.

You begin to ask yourself as you look at the front page, or

the third page, or any page, "Is God really in control?" Perhaps
the only good news on the front page is that the home team won.
And if He's in control when they win, is He out of control when
they lose?

There's not one of us who has not asked such questions as,
"Who's in control? Why is this happening? Where's God? Why
doesn't He do something about all this tragedy?" You see, for
centuries the presence of suffering and moral evil has caused what
I call "the great conversation" or the great debate. Men have faced
this question long before you and I were brought into the world.

Epicurus, one of the Greek philosophers said this: "God either
wishes to take away evil and is unable, or He is able and unwilling.
Or He is neither willing nor able. Or He is both willing and able.
Now if He is willing but unable, He is a feeble God. If He is
able and unwilling, He is envious. If He is neither willing nor
able, He is both envious and feeble, and therefore is not God.
And if He is both willing and able, which alone is suitable for
God, why doesn't He remove evil from our society?" Good question.
Let's think about it for awhile. Rabbi Harold Kushner wrote a
book in 1984 titled, *Why Bad Things Happen to Good People.*
The Rabbi basically tries to explain why tragic things can befall
good people. I suppose it is easier for us to understand why bad
things happen to bad people. But why do bad things happen to
good people? Rabbi Kushner's book became a best seller, but as
a Christian I totally disagreed with his thesis.

Basically, Kushner said this: Bad things happen to good people
because God is limited and is unable at times to get into the daily
affairs of men and really straighten things out. I have a terrible
problem with that, biblically and theologically. I happen to believe
that my God has always been on the throne. I don't think He's
gone on vacation. I don't think He has taken a sick leave. I don't
believe He's off the throne and somebody else is representing Him
by proxy. And I have a difficult time with a "limited God" concept.

The validity of our faith stems from its object, not its intensity.
We can be intense in our faith, and we can believe a lot of things
yet be totally wrong. It's our object of faith, not our intensity of
faith, that gives us a valid faith. If I have a limited God, and my
God is somehow in the process of becoming a great God but He
isn't quite there yet, I'm in trouble! Because if I have a limited
God, I also have at best a limited faith. My faith is totally
contingent upon Him and His ability to work on my behalf in my life.

If I have a limited God, it affects my worship. When I look into the Old and New Testament, I find that the men of God's Word did not have a "limited God" concept. Read Isaiah 40 and you'll see what that prophet says about God. You'll realize he didn't think he had a God who was hard of hearing, or decrepit.

If I believe that I have a limited God, it affects my prayer life. How do you pray to a limited God? What promises will He answer? What promises *can* He answer? Do I ask that He try to help me to the best of His limited ability? What nonsense such an exercise would be. The belief in a limited God not only limits my worship and my prayer life, it also limits my character. If God is in the process of becoming better, how in the world will I ever become righteous? There would be an absolute ceiling upon the possibility or potential of my growth if I worship a God who is stunted spiritually, ethically, morally or in His attributes. That's why I have problems believing anything so shallow.

There are many great men of the Bible who praised and lifted up God in His fullness. One of my favorite prophets is Habakkuk. Habakkuk watched his country literally being raped and plundered and destroyed by Babylon, an idolatrous country. They were under the judgment of God. Habakkuk talks about seeing the judgment of God, hearing it, feeling it, experiencing it. If there was anybody who might sit down and say, "Wait a minute, is God in control? What's happening here?" it would be Habakkuk. This passage of Scripture is the strongest passage in all of God's Word, concerning faith. After seeing all of the wrong things happen to the right people, Habakkuk says, "Though the fig tree does not bud and there are no grapes on the vines, though the olive crop fails and the fields produce no food, though there are no sheep in the pen and no cattle in the stalls, yet I will rejoice in the Lord, I will be joyful in God my Savior. The sovereign Lord is my strength; he makes my feet like the feet of a deer, and he enables me to go on to the heights" (3:17-19, NIV). How's that for amazing faith?

In our more contemporary times we might say, "Though the stock market crashes and there is no money in the banks, though the supply of fuel dwindles and the machinery of society grinds to a halt, though our ecological blunders ruin the crops and there are barren shelves in the market, yet I will rejoice in the Lord. I will be joyful in God my Savior."

There comes a time in life when we have to decide something. We have to decide whether or not we believe God is on the throne when things displease us in our lives. And we have to decide whether we're going to trust Him because He is a sovereign and omnipotent God, or whether we're going to get shaken every time the headlines don't proclaim glad tidings. Where are we going to put our faith? In the local newspaper or in the Bible?

I love to read Romans 11:33-36: "Oh, the depth of the riches both of the wisdom and knowledge of God! How unsearchable are His judgments and unfathomable His ways! For who has known the mind of the Lord, or who became His counselor? Or who has first given to Him that it might be paid back to Him again? For from Him and through Him and to Him are all things. To Him be the glory forever. Amen." Paul obviously did not have a concept of a "limited God "

Read Revelation 15:3-4. John did not have a limited God concept either. Now if there was anybody who might have a right to be a bit shaken up, it was John. All of his colleagues had been killed for their faith. John was tortured, then banished to an island. He was left there all alone. He was in his last years of life. The power of the Roman empire was stronger than it ever had been before. As John sat down on the isle of Patmos, I think it would be very honest and truthful to say that there had to come to his mind the question, "Is truth on the scaffold? Is it ready to be hung? Is it about to have its ending?" Truly, if any man were qualified to ask the question, "Why do bad things happen to good people?" it would be John. But listen to his words in Revelation 15:3-4: "Great and marvelous are Thy works, O Lord God, the Almighty; righteous and true are Thy ways, Thou King of the nations. Who will not fear, O Lord, and glorify Thy name? For Thou alone art holy; for all the nations will come and worship before Thee, for Thy righteous acts have been revealed."

When I start reading my Bible, I ask myself this question: How did these Bible characters develop such a faith in a God that was in control when things around them seemed to be out of control? Over the years I've discovered answers to my question.

1. God *Is* Greater Than Evil and Will One Day Triumph Over It.

I think the apostles understood that. One day He will triumph over evil entirely. That doesn't mean that God is losing. It means that God has not yet unleashed His final battle against evil. It's coming. Don't get discouraged. Turn to Revelation 21. Have you ever read a book and wondered how things are going to turn out? Have you ever gone to the last page in the book to find out?

I love the story about the boy who was up one night reading a Western novel, all worried about his favorite hero. His mother came in and wanted him to go to bed but he was upset because his hero was all tied up and the boy wasn't sure if the hero was going to survive. The mother pleaded with him to put the book aside and go to bed. But he couldn't do that. About ten minutes later he had a big smile on his face and his mother asked what happened. The boy replied, "Mommy, I couldn't handle it anymore. I went to the last page of the book and the hero wins and rides off gloriously into the sunset. The villian is shot and done forever." And later as he went back and read the rest of the book, he kept telling the good guy, "If only you knew what I know."

When I read the Bible I keep saying the same thing. And I'm sure that John thought, "I know that Rome is in control now. I know that they are making a path across the world. I know that they are denying the read God. I know I'm only one man on the isle of Patmos and I'm banished out here and I don't look too strong. And I know the town criers aren't going to come out here and do an article on me. But I also know it's all right. I know who is going to win in the end."

All the great men in God's Word understand something. They understand that God is going to win. Look at Revelation 21:1-7: "And I saw a new heaven and a new earth; for the first heaven and the first earth passed away, and there is no longer any sea." And there are no longer any depressing headlines in our local newspaper. "And I saw the holy city, new Jerusalem, coming down out of heaven from God, made ready as a bride adorned for her husband. And I heard a loud voice from the throne, saying, 'Behold, the tabernacle of God is among men, and He shall dwell among them, and they shall be His people, and God Himself shall be among them, and He shall wipe away every tear from their eyes; and there shall no longer be any death; there shall no longer be any mourning, or crying, or pain; the first things have passed away.' And He who sits on the throne said, 'Behold, I am making all things new.' And He said, 'Write, for these words are faithful and true,' And He said to me, 'It is done. I am the Alpha and the Omega, the beginning and the end. I will give to the one who thirsts from the spring of the water of life without cost. He who

overcomes shall inherit these things, and I will be his God and
he will be My son.'"

That's your promise. It helps us begin to understand that as
God's children, we'll still read the paper, still get blue, still get
miserable (the writers will make sure that we get somewhat miserable
at least), but we won't hold our breath about whether or not the
Padres win today. We won't bite our fingernails down to the bone
concerning the GOP convention. We will understand that our God
is a big God, and in the presence of an evil world, in spite of
all of the many problems, He still has the ability to work out His
will for man. Satan thought he had Him fixed at the cross, didn't
he? He died and Satan in hell jumped for joy. The disciples cowered
off to a room and locked the door and thought it was over. But
God in His omnipotence looked down upon a confused, frustrated
world and on the third day said, "Son, rise up." We just can't see
the other side. We're so impatient. "Oh, Lord, I've got a problem,"
we pray, "and I know You're busy so I'll give You a whole five
seconds to answer this problem." Would that we could gain more
spiritual maturity and patience.

2. God Will Not Do Anything That Is Contrary to His Own Nature.

He will not manipulate people as robots. He also won't violate
our own freedom of choice. He gives us the freedom to enjoy or
suffer the consequences. In His sovereignty there are some things
He has chosen not to interfere with. He has given us a free will
so that we can have genuine fellowship with Him. Without this
free will, we would be no more loving than a computer screen
which prints out "I love you" when you program it to do so. God
does not want a dictated relationship. He wants us to choose to
love Him. Regrettably, our free will gives us the latitude to be
violent, reckless, and evil. It's not that God isn't in control, it's
a matter of us being purposely out of control.

3. As Christians, We Need to Understand the Purpose of Life.

The apostles were able to smile through adversity because they
did not have an American culture or mind-set concerning God's
purpose for their lives. They didn't have a happiness mind-set.
They didn't think God was incredibly disturbed until we put on a

happy face. They understood the whole process of life and God's purpose.

There is a Roman proverb that says, "When you do not know what port you are headed for, any wind is a bad one." When you do not know what your purpose in life is, I promise you, every wind is a wind of adversity. You won't know where you are, nor where you are headed, nor where you have been. Unless we know God's purpose for our lives, unless we know what God has planned for us, we will never be able to sit down and distinguish the difference between what is good and what is bad for us. Nietzche said, "If we have our own 'why' of life we shall get along with almost any 'how.'" So, when somebody says something good happens to them or something bad happens to them, I wonder if they understand what the purpose of it all is.

4. God's Purpose Is Different for Each of His Children.

God's plan for your life is not the same as God's plan for my life. True, there are some general purposes we all share: our salvation, our holiness, our worship of God. Those, however, are the general purposes of all mankind. Beyond that, there are some specific purposes or plans He has for me that He does not have for you. And there are some that He has for you that He does not have for me. We get into trouble when we question the "bad" things that happen to us. We sit down on our sanctified stools and begin to sulk, and ask ourselves, "Why did this happen to me and not to him? I love God as much as he does. Why do I get all the bad breaks?"

John 21 is an example of this situation. Remember when Jesus came to Peter and asked, "Do you love me?"? Peter always answered yes. After the third time Jesus asked the same question, He went on to explain that Peter would henceforth be abused and scoffed and treated harshly because of his belief in Christ. Eventually, that is what happened. Peter died after being crucified upside down.

But when Jesus told Peter what would happen, Peter pointed to John and asked, "What about him?"

Do you know what he was saying? "Lord, I don't mind dying for you as long as the rest of these fellows die, too. Be fair."

And what did the Lord say to Peter? "Peter, it's none of your

business! [Maxwell translation.] It's none of your business what
I'm going to do with John. John's going to live on the isle of Patmos.
John's not going to die a martyr's death. He'll be the only one of
the twelve who will not. But don't worry about him." Then He
looked at Peter and said, "You follow Me." In other words, He
said, "John and Peter, you two men have the same Lord, but you
don't have the same missions for your lives. Do what you are
called to do, and don't be looking over your shoulder to see what
someone else is doing."

Peter's real problem was less one of jealousy of John than a
bafflement over why the specific ordeals Christ spoke of should
befall him, particularly. He had been loyal to Christ, had served
as leader of the apostles, had been a faithful worker. Why then
should such forthcoming anguish and turmoil befall him? Was it
logical?

Is suffering logical, ever? Can the believer rely on nothing?
Will the just suffer as much, if not more, than the unjust?

These are ageless questions. Man has pondered them for centuries. Yet, there are answers. The answers are also ageless. For
that reason, we'll focus on one of the oldest recorded incidents
of supposedly undeserved ill treatment ever received by a God-fear-
ing person: the life of Job.

The discipline, character strength, fortitude and humility of Job
help us to gain a special perspective of human suffering. There
are six important conclusions which we can draw from a study of
Job. Let's review them now:

1. *Being righteous does not eliminate problems.*

Frequently, you will hear someone say that people suffer because
they are being punished for their sins. That is not necessarily true.
Suffering, indeed, can be caused by sin, but it can be the result
of other factors, too.

In the opening words of the Book of Job we read, "There was
a man in the land of Uz, whose name was Job, and that man
was blameless, upright, fearing God, and turning away from evil."
That is a pretty positive statement to make about a man. Job was
a good man. You see, the Bible wants us to know that before we
learn about his suffering and his trials. This man who will have
everything go wrong in his life, is a super-good guy! Don't let
anybody put you on a guilt trip that says if you've got a problem
it's because you've sinned and you need to check your spiritual
pulse every day. If there is sin, ask for forgiveness. In our society

of evil, bad things can happen to you that are no direct result of your sins.

2. *Having problems come our way does not mean that God is not in control.*

Just because you have problems and bad days, that does not mean that God has gone on a vacation. Not only does the Bible begin this chapter by saying that Job was an upright man, it also points out that God was on the throne. Satan came to ask God for permission to tempt Job. The one who gives permission is the one who is in control.

3. *We must be honest with ourselves and with God when we have problems.*

We need to be more transparent. When Job had problems he didn't say, "Well, everything is fine." He looked at God and said, "There are some things I don't understand." Listen to his words: "And should my head be lifted up, Thou wouldst hunt me like a lion; and again Thou wouldst show Thy power against me" (10:16). In Job 7:12, "Am I the sea, or the sea monster, that Thou dost set a guard over me?" Job never questioned his suffering. He only questioned the extent of his suffering. No questions arise from Job until he is incredibly plagued. Only then does he start to ask why.

4. *God's purpose is often hidden from us.*

The reason Job questioned so much was that he did not understand God's purpose for his life. That's obvious. The Book of Job talks about God being judicial. God is the judge. Job says he wishes he had an attorney or an arbitrator, so they could start communication flowing. He did not understand what God's purpose was. One of the great things about the Word of God is this: Job was God's first example of trials for the Christian world. And the questions that Job pondered were much graver than what we have gone through because Job didn't have anyone else to look to as an example of how God worked in his life. Job was the first project of God. The joy I have is the fact that every time I go through this process I can go back to Job and observe what God did in Job's life. Then I can begin to see purpose more easily in my life.

5. *Beware of "cut and dry" theologies that reduce the ways of God into a manageable formula.*

That's what Job's friends tried to do. They tried to take their experiences (beware of all experiential theology) and put them on Job. They had a "commercial view of faith." What I mean is this:

Commercial views of faith say that if you serve God He will give you only good things. If you do not serve God, He will give you bad things. That's not true.

Scripture tells us that the rain falls on the unjust and the just. Because of this, false ministers have real problems in the whole area of Job and his faith. When you have trouble like Job had and you have a commercial faith, you have two ways to go: You can say, "God, You have done me wrong. I'm Your child, so why would these things be happening to me? God, change my situation and problems." Or, you can just curse God, get mad and walk away. That's what Job's wife told him to do. You only have those two options.

6. *Look for a better relationship with God instead of reasons for your problems.*

The most important thing that can be said about Job's life is that while his friends were looking for reasons for his problems, Job was concerned about his relationship with God. He never questioned God's sovereignty. God was on the throne in the beginning of Job, and God would be on the throne at the end of Job. God never moved. Just the circumstances of a man changed.

The word "almighty" is used 48 times in the Bible in the Old Testament. In the Book of Job it's used 31 times alone. Job never questioned God's power, God's strength, God's ability.

At the beginning of his suffering, Job expressed confidence in the greatness of God. "His wisdom is profound, his power is vast . . .He alone stretched out the heavens and treads on the waves of the sea. . .He performs wonders that cannot be fathomed, miracles that cannot be numbered." At the close of his trial, Job still believed in the greatness of God: "I know that Thou canst do all things, and that no purpose of Thine can be thwarted."

Have you watched the TV game shows that give the viewer the answer on the screen while it is unknown to the participant? The show host gives hints and you sit in the living room wondering why the player does not immediately come up with the answer. It's so simple from your viewpoint. The hints are logical and certainly the answer is apparent. Why is the contestant struggling to find an answer? Where is his confidence? When will the "light" break through?

In the game of life we are the participants. Paul, in 1 Corinthians 13:12, says, "For now we see in a mirror dimly, but then face to face; now I know in part, but then I shall know fully just as I also have been fully known."

CHAPTER 11

Can Christ Use My Failures?

The Bible talks much about some of its greatest men. Abraham is known as a "friend of God." Jacob, who wrestled all night long with the angel, had his name changed to Israel. As a prince, Jacob prevailed and had power, the Bible says, with God. Moses, unquestionably the greatest leader of the Old Testament, spoke with God directly. Probably no man in the Bible had more influence with God than he. David was a man after God's own heart.

If we go into the New Testament, we see Peter, whom Jesus looked to for leadership qualities. He not only referred to Peter as the rock upon which He would build His church, He also said, "I will give you the keys of the kingdom of heaven" (Matt. 16:19). The apostle Paul, the great leader of the New Testament, was called God's chosen instrument.

These men, plus many others, have two things in common. One, obviously, is they were all great men of God, and were greatly used of God. The second thing is that, at some time in their lives, they all failed God miserably. Every one of them. Abraham lied. Jacob was deceitful. Moses disobeyed God. David committed adultery. Peter denied he ever knew Christ or that he was one of the disciples. And, of course, Paul was described by himself as the chief of all sinners, a murderer. They were all great men of God, but they also all failed God in incredible ways.

The word failure is a dirty word to us. The thought of failure terrorizes us. When we see it, hear it, or find ourselves being a part of it we want to hide from it, run from it, deny it. We want to do everything we can with the word "failure" except accept it.

When I study the lives of great men in history, I notice the common strand of failure within their lives, too. When Enrico Caruso, the great Italian tenor, took his first voice lesson, the instructor shook his head and said that his voice sounded like wind whistling through a window. Henry Ford forgot to put a reverse gear in the first car he invented. Also, he didn't build a door wide enough to get the car out of the building he built the car in. If you go to Greenfield Village, you can see where he cut a hole in the wall to get the car out. Thomas Edison, known as the greatest of inventors, spent $2 million on one invention and never did invent what he wanted. In fact, that great man got many of his inventions from other less dedicated inventors who had tried and quit. He would work on their ideas until he perfected them. He invented a battery that is used in submarines today. But he experimented with it correcting thousands of failures before he finally perfected it.

Abraham Lincoln, whom we admire so much, lived a life riddled with failure. In 1831 Lincoln failed in business; in 1832 he was defeated in the election for the Illinois state legislature; in 1833 he again failed in business; in 1834 he was elected to the legislature, but in 1835 his fiancée died; in 1838 he was defeated for house speaker; in 1840 he was defeated for elector; in 1842 he did marry, but his wife proved to be a sickly and mentally depressed woman. Lincoln was defeated for congress in 1843. He was elected to congress in 1846 but lost his run for congress in 1848. He was defeated for the senate in 1855. He was defeated for vice-president in 1856. He was defeated again for the senate in 1858. And in 1860 he was elected President. The man's life was literally checkered with failure. Nevertheless, today he is recognized as one of the greatest of all our Presidents. Lincoln proved that it is not what happens to us, but what happens in us, that makes us either a failure or a success. This applies to our Christian walk, too.

When I think of sin in the context of, "Can Christ use my failures?" my mind is immediately drawn to the story of David. In regard to sinful failings, we must remember that this does not refer to the failure to make wise purchases or the failures to get a meal to turn out right. Instead, we are strictly referring to the failure to obey God's statutes and to walk in His steps. That was

David's problem.

Let's look at David's life. Saul was king before David. Saul's failures never seemed as drastic or terrible as David's. Both men were so similar. Both were warrior kings; both were anointed by God; both were chosen by God for great deeds; both sinned; both were reproached for their sin; yet one died in disgrace (Saul) and the other died with the glory of God upon his life (David). As God's people, it is not what happens to us, but what happens in us, that determines whether or not we are failures.

Second Samuel 12 tells us that David's men were in battle, yet David was back in Jerusalem. One day David looked across the courtyard and saw a beautiful woman, Bathsheba, and he lusted for her. Bathsheba was married to a soldier named Uriah. David summoned her to the palace and seduced her. Later, Nathan the prophet came to David to confront him about his sin of adultery. There are eight events in David's life that help us understand what we should do if we fail or sin against God as he did.

1. *We must accept a confrontation with our sin.* The first thing that happened in David's life after he failed God was that God was faithful to him. The Bible says in 2 Samuel 12, "Then the Lord sent Nathan." What an interesting phrase, "Then the Lord sent Nathan to David." When did God send the prophet to the king? When David had sinned. Look at 2 Samuel 11:27: "But the thing that David had done was evil in the sight of the Lord." It was when David had sinned and failed God that God sent Nathan to David. God won't allow us to sin without sending checks into our lives. It is a biblical principle. We cannot sin continually without having God send people, situations, or circumstances into our lives to wave red warning flags and say, "You are going down the wrong road." God is merciful and kind and caring toward us. Nathan walked into the palace one day and confronted David with his sin.

We know Nathan's story of a poor man who had only one lamb and a rich man who, instead of using some of his own flock, went over and took the poor man's lamb and sacrificed it to provide a meal for his friends.

After Nathan told David this story, David's anger burned greatly against the rich man. He said to Nathan, "As the Lord lives, surely the man who has done this deserves to die." It was easier for David to see other's failures than to see his own. As long as Nathan referred to other people, David was able to say, "My goodness, that's terrible." We are more harsh on other people's failures than on our own. David was ready to kill the rich man for taking the lamb.

However, Nathan then said to David, "You are the man. Thus says the Lord God of Israel, 'It is I who anointed you king over Israel and it is I who delivered you from the hand of Saul.'" Nathan then revealed that David had arranged for Uriah to be murdered. Nathan proclaimed, "Thus says the Lord, 'Behold I will raise up evil against you from your own household.'" From that moment on, David had incredible problems in his home with his sons and his wives. There was constant insurrection because of his sin.

The point is, when we fail God, God is faithful to us, bringing people or situations into our lives to confront us and let us know we are sinning and failing God. It is impossible for a believer to continue to sin against God and not know he or she is sinning. God is faithful to you and will speak to you about the failures in your life.

2. *We must admit we have done wrong.* David openly admitted to Nathan and to God that he had done wrong: "Then David said to Nathan, 'I have sinned against the Lord.'" Nathan said to David, "The Lord also has taken away your sin; you shall not die."

What we usually do when we sin against God is to hide the sin or rationalize it or blame someone else for it. In David's situation, however, he admitted that he had done wrong. Our first failure against God is not what sinks us spiritually. It is our second failure. When God shows us our first failure, our human tendency is to deny it or excuse it or white-wash it. That is the greater failure. The worst failure is not the sin against God, but our negative reaction to God when He begins to deal with us about that sin in our life. David agreed with Nathan.

Remember that David's first sin was committing adultery and murdering Uriah. The second sin that blighted the career of David was the taking of a census. David had become a victorious king over many enemies. Pride lifted him up, and he wanted to take a census to see how many people he ruled over. We read in 1 Chronicles 21:1, "Then Satan stood up against Israel and moved David to number Israel." That is an interesting phrase. After David had defeated his worldly enemies, he was confronted by Satan. He had to do battle with him. Many times when we become successful in our walk with God and we begin to have a few victories, it is then that Satan rises up and begins to challenge us. That's when we begin to fight not against flesh and blood, but against spiritual powers.

3. *We must accept responsibility for our failures.* David took responsibility for his sin. He didn't blame Bathsheba by saying something like, "It's really her fault, she was indecently exposed. I couldn't help myself." No, he took the responsibility for his sin. God will never be able to do His work in our lives concerning failure and sin until we quit blaming our mom, dad, brothers, sisters, wife, or husband, and we say, "It's me, it's me, it's me, O Lord, standing in the need of prayer." It's me.

4. *We must trust in God's mercy.* David knew that he had disappointed God and that, both as a man and as a king he had failed God. Yet, he fasted and prayed, knowing that God was forgiving and merciful. He arose from his three days of repenting, justified and forgiven.

5. *We must show sincerity toward God.* David demonstrated his sincerity toward God. The Bible says he fasted. He laid on the ground all night. The elders of his household stood beside him through the night trying to raise him up from the ground, but he was unwilling and would not eat food with them. In other words, he showed sincere repentance. He was sorry for what he had done. He demonstrated that by fasting and prayer. It hurt him that he had hurt God.

6. *We must renew our fellowship with God.* It's not enough just to feel bad for what we've done. There has to be a renewal of fellowship. The Bible says that after his repentance David arose from the ground and washed and anointed himself and came to the house of the Lord and worshipped the Lord. When we fail God, we have the tendency to leave church, our Christian friends and our Christian influence and to hide in the corner and try to nurse ourselves back. David, when he sinned against God, said he would go back and pray to renew fellowship with the Lord.

7. *We must change our attitudes.* After his failure, David underwent a great change in his life. It all began with a change of attitude. David arose from the ground, he washed and anointed himself, he changed his clothes, he ate. His servant said, "What is this thing that you have done? While the child was alive, you fasted and wept; but when the child died, you arose and ate food." David was demonstrating that he couldn't look back. What had happened had happened and now he needed to regroup, change

his clothes, wash himself outwardly and wash himself inwardly. There needed to be an entire change of mind-set. David was showing that he was sorry for what he had done, he showed repentance, and how he had to begin again by changing his attitudes. He had to understand that God forgave him. He had to go back to attending to the job God originally assigned him to do.

8. *We must look to the future.* After the death of their illegitimate child, David comforted his wife. He then put his grief for the child behind him: "Now he has died; why should I fast? Can I bring him back again? I shall go to him, but he will not return to me." David began to look to the future. It was time to sire a legitimate heir. The Bible says, "Then David comforted his wife, Bathsheba, and went in to her and lay with her; and she gave birth to a son, and he named him Solomon. Now the Lord loved him." This was the new beginning. Because of David's futuristic outlook, Israel would soon enter the greatest era of its history.

When David sinned in numbering the people, God said he was going to give David a choice of three punishments: ". . .'three years of famine, or three months to be swept away before your foes, while the sword of your enemies overtakes you, or else three days of the sword of the Lord, even pestilence in the land, and the angel of the Lord destroying throughout all the territory of Israel.' Now therefore, consider what answer I shall return to him who sent me."

David said to God, "I am in great distress. Please let me fall into the hand of the Lord, for His mercies are very great. But do not let me fall into the hand of man." Powerful. David, when he was confronted, said he would rather trust in the mercies of God. He asked not to fall into the hands of man; man would judge harshly; man would not forgive; man would continue to remember what David had done in the past. David chose to fall into the hands of God. We think of the Old Testament as the book of the law. An eye for an eye and a tooth for a tooth. But here David, in his understanding of failure, said he would rather fall into the hands of God, who is merciful and kind and forgiving and loves with an unqualified love, than to fall into the hands of man.

When you fail God, the best recourse is for you to turn and not just look, but to run head-long as fast as you can back to the God you have failed, rejected, disappointed, and disobeyed. You must thrust your whole life and body and failures into the arms of the loving, merciful, kind, compassionate and forgiving God.

Go to Him. He loves you. He is an expert in dealing with failure. He's handled it "all His life." He's had practice with Abraham, Moses, David, Peter, and Paul.

Let's note one final important episode in David's life. After David had sinned by ordering the census, he went to a man, a farmer, who had a piece of ground. It was on that piece of ground that David wanted to offer a sacrifice to God for his failure. The farmer was willing to give it to King David. But David said, "No, I won't offer to God anything that is free. I will only offer to God that which I have paid for. I'm not going to come to God with a free sacrifice. I'll pay my part." And he did. He bought the ground. Here's the conclusion: In David's first sin he married Bathsheba and out of that wrong relationship over which David repented, they had a son by the name of Solomon. The Bible says that God loved Solomon. He became the next king of Israel. The piece of ground that David bought after he committed his second great sin was the ground upon which Solomon built the Temple. See the picture? God took the two greatest failures in David's life, adultery with Bathsheba and the taking of a census, and turned them into blessings.

If God can do that for David, don't you think He can take the biggest mistakes that you've made and turn them around for His glory? David demonstrates to us that our attitude, not our sin, is the determining factor of whether our failures make or break us. To accept failure as something final is to finally fail.

CHAPTER 12

Why Do Children Stray From God?

One night I put my son, Joel Porter, to bed. Typical of a child, he kept getting up for a glass of water and to go to the bathroom. Finally, after the seventh time, I warned him not to get up again. I also promised him that if he got out of his bed that I would have to discipline him. A few moments later, while sitting in the family room, I could tell he was once again out of bed. From the sounds of things, it seemed like he was doing a one and a half twist off his dresser onto the bed. Knowing I would have to follow through on my warning to him, I began walking toward the bedroom.

Our hallway is tiled so he could hear me coming. As I turned the corner and looked into his bedroom I saw him fly for his bed, Superman style, as fast as possible. In one motion he grabbed his pillow, rolled over on his back, stuck his thumb in his mouth, and closed his eyes as if he were sleeping. I walked into the room and just stood there waiting for him to open his eyes. Remember when you were a child and had done something wrong and were pretending to be asleep? It would not be long before you would have to open your eyes. When Joel opened his eyes he knew he was in trouble. Immediately he opened up both arms, looked at me and smiled and said, "Daddy, let's pray." You guessed it. . . we prayed. I left the room as fast as possible to keep from laughing. It's amazing how creative children can become when facing the valley of the shadow of death.

In one of her weaker moments, my wife Margaret said to me,
"Do you think we ought to adopt one more child?" I smiled and
said, "Well, let's think about it." Inwardly, I was gripped with
fear. *Oh, God, help us.* But the Lord incredibly answers prayer.
Recently, during District Conference, some of our friends came
down and stayed with us. They have a little two-year-old who
reminded us of Joel Porter two years ago. My wife reports now
that she thinks we have had alpha and omega. It removed all of
her questions. She's content with just two children.

Kids are really great. Probably the greatest joys you have in
life center on your kids. Unfortunately, some of the greatest hurts
that you have in life are also centered on them. You can go to
your favorite Christian bookstore and I'll guarantee that you'll find
dozens of books on marriage, family, the home, and how to
discipline children. In fact, sometimes they can confuse you because
you can pull three or four of them off the rack and they will tell
you to do contrasting things. Deciding is not easy. The books give
you good, practical help on family life but very seldom deal with
how to help parents whose junior didn't "turn out" like they hoped
he would.

We feel guilty. We've all heard the message from Proverbs 22:6.
"Train up a child in the way he should go: and when he is old,
he will not depart from it" (KJV). And every time we think of
our child who is not living like we would desire, we ask ourselves,
"What did I do wrong?" We feel frustrated.

Sometimes we feel like the mother who heard the doorbell ring
and went to answer the door. It was somebody who was trying
to raise money for a children's home in the community. The fellow
said, "Ma'am, I hope you will give us all that you can." She
replied, "Yes, I've got two of them right here. You can have them
both." When we feel this way, we sense guilt. We feel
frustrated when our family does not operate like the old television
show, "Father Knows Best." Perhaps what is shared in this chapter
will help all of us.

WHO'S AT FAULT?

When our kids don't turn out like we expected, who do we
blame on? Every family has those crisis points when the children
don't function the way we feel they should. We see signs of
disobedience and rebellion within the ranks. We begin to look at

our youngsters and see that they have wills of their own. They often make decisions that are contrary to what you and I would like to see them make. Fear grips the hearts of parents as they begin to see children making wrong decisions.

The other day I was having a meal with Jim and Annie Jackson. Annie is finishing a Ph.D. in child relationships. I thought it would be a good time to talk to her about the make-up of a child.

I asked Annie, "What is it that makes children turn out as they do?" She said something quite interesting. "A child's environment, plus what he has done with what he has."

I quickly wrote that down and I've developed a formula from that statement. She said the environment of the child, plus his experiences, plus the equipping of that child, really make up that young person. As I began to study that, I began to think about our environment. Parents have a great deal of input on the environment as well as the experiences they provide for their children. Obviously, peer pressure in society also has a lot of impact.

I thought of the equipping — the stuff that God put in us that makes us "us." He wired us differently, didn't He? Have you ever wondered why everyone in the world can't be like you? Have you ever thought about that — why they aren't smart, quick, intelligent, nice and kind, like you? That equipping work of God really makes us unique. I began to ask myself, if environment, experience and equipping make up the person, then who's at fault if the person doesn't turn out as he's supposed to?

First of all, let's see what *common sense* would say. I have seen what I would consider to be outstanding Christian parents who have had children who did not turn out as they should. I have also seen what I consider to be bad parents — people who do not go to church, who do not love God, who never read the Bible, who provide a terrible environment — and yet their children come from that environment, turn their lives over to God, and become church leaders. They'll make statements like this, "I saw what alcohol did to my parents so I'll never touch it." It's almost as though that bad environment turned them and kicked them out into something that was secure and solid and sound.

I've seen good parents with bad kids and bad parents with good kids. Then I've seen good parents with two kids, one good and one not so good. When I begin to look and analyze that, common sense tells me that parents probably do have the greatest influence on their children, but parents are not the only influence on their children.

How much guilt should we, as parents, carry around when our kids are really not doing what we want them to do? Should we lament, "If only I would have done this right or I would have changed that." Actually, no. The fact is that no matter what influence we exert over our children, we will never be able to suppress their free will. As such, we cannot bear the total burden of responsibility for their waywardness.

Common sense tells me, "More than likely good parenting produces good children. And more than likely bad parenting produces bad kids, but there are many exceptions to the rule."

Secondly, what does *science* say about this? Time doesn't allow me to talk about psychology and sociology and anthropology and other areas of science. But anthropology has proven that different cultures produce different types of people. We don't even need to go to a foreign land to learn that. We can see it in the United States.

When you travel you find that people are different in various areas of the country. They talk with different accents, they wear different kinds of clothes, they prefer different types of food, they reflect various ethnic heritages, and they engage in different kinds of hobbies, sports and social activities. These cultural and regional characteristics will have an impact on young people growing up in those areas.

Anthropology and sociology teach us that a lot of what we are is because of the culture in which we have been raised. So, science would basically tell us that, no, it is not just the parents who are to blame if children don't turn out right. We must also weigh the influence of television, radio, school, magazines, newspapers, church, relatives, friends, and neighbors.

BIBLICAL PERSPECTIVE

Look at Proverbs 22:6: "Train up a child in the way he should go." Wow. I want to be very careful in this part of the chapter because you know how I respect God's Word. I love to preach expositionally from His Word, but I want to teach you something specific in this book. Different books in the Bible have different purposes. There are the prophetic books, historical books, and wisdom literature.

The wisdom literature is composed of observations of wise men inspired by God concerning life. I think we have looked at Proverbs

22:6 for way too long as an irrevocable promise, when in reality
it is an observation of a wise man. I sometimes cringe when I
see Christians handle the Word of God, claiming promises that are
not promises, and latching on to scriptural truths out of context
that make them untrue. You can prove anything in the Bible if
you just take a verse or an isolated passage of Scripture. You have
to look to the whole and Proverbs is a group of wise men making
wise sayings. The observation is beautiful. The wise man says, if
you train up a child in the way he should go, even when he is
old he will not depart from it. In other words, as a general rule,
the training of your child will determine the outcome of your child.

I know you're saying, "Pastor, I look at verse 6 and I don't
see the word *usually* in there. You're adding the word."

I would say, "That's right." But I would also have you notice
that I am adding a word if I say, "Train up a child in the way
he should go and *invariably* he shall not depart from it." What
we have to understand is that this is an observation we need to
commit ourselves to, and to follow.

I am not trying to absolve parents from the responsibility to
train their children. All parents should feel keenly responsible. I'm
just trying to relieve what I call false guilt. Parents run around as
if everything junior did depended upon them. Most parents can't
even *think up* some of the things junior did!

Parents must learn to have a proper perspective on child- rearing.
If you are going to take Proverbs 22:6 as an irrevocable, invariable
promise that never changes, what are you going to do with
Proverbs 2:1? Proverbs reminds us that even the very best training
may not be sufficient. What I like about Proverbs 2:1 is that it
places the responsibility on the child. It begins, "my son, if [I
want you to circle that word *if]* you will receive my sayings, and
treasure my commandments within you, make your ear attentive
to wisdom, incline your heart to understanding; for if [circle that
word *if* again] you cry for discernment, lift your voice for understanding; if [circle that word] you seek her as silver [that's three
if's], and search for her as for hidden treasures; *then* you will
discern the fear of the Lord and discover the knowledge of God."

The writer in Proverbs 2:1 is just making another observation.
This is not for parents, but for children. He is saying that if
children listen to what their parents say and observe and accept
that advice, then they will find the wisdom and the way of God.
It's another observation. Not an irrevocable promise, just an obser-

vation, and an admonition to children that part of their development welfare rests on their own shoulders.

IN THE BEGINNING

Let's go back to the beginning. God created Adam in His image. Have you ever thought about God and His creation and the privilege He gave Adam of having a choice, a will? God gave Adam an ideal environment and an opportunity to be a godly person. There was no communication gap between God and Adam. God came down regularly and had communion and fellowship with Adam.

Adam knew what his rules of conduct were. God had explained everything clearly. Every tree in the garden except one was for Adam. Communication was clear. Fellowship was continual. But Adam had a choice, and he decided to do his own thing regardless of what God said. Adam rebelled. So now, shall we say that God was a bad parent?

God in His creation gave us a will to choose. Basically God tells us as parents that we can pray, "God, keep my children from the great temptations of life, and when they fall deliver them. Help my child to marry a good spouse." But there is one thing we cannot do and that is force God to save our children. We can create the right kind of environment, we can pray and weep, do everything possible. We must realize that the Bible teaches us through general observation, "If we train up a child in the way he should go. . .he will not depart from it," but we cannot bank on that as an irrevocable promise. It comes down to the fact that the child has a will and an ability to choose. That fact cannot be altered.

This free will of a child's is impacted by an era of confusion regarding *how* a child or young adult should behave these days. Most young people have no idea when they are supposed to start assuming adult responsibilities. Things are not as cut and dried today as they were in other eras.

In his book *Staying Ahead of Time* (R & R Newkirk, 1981), Dr. Dennis E. Hensley explains this contemporary phenomenon:

> The adolescent stage of our lives takes us from childhood to adulthood. In the past, many societies have had specific ways by which to determine when adulthood was reached. African tribes held rites of passage. American Indians required boys to accomplish tasks and endure ordeals to prove manhood. In our colonial days, a boy was considered an adult once he finished

his apprenticeship and could work; a girl was considered a woman once she married.

Today, however, our society is less regimented. We don't seem to know anymore just when adulthood is reached. We do make random attempts to establish age values. We will allow no one to drive until age 16, allow no one to vote until 18, allow no one to run for office until 21, and allow no one to serve as President until 35. The range here is obviously great. It seems to underscore the fact that maturity and age are not necessarily one and the same (pp. 10-11).

Some children do not live up to our expectations, because they can't figure out what our expectations are. They are more confused than we are.

WHAT CAN I DO?

Whether parents believe it or not, most children do want to please them. The problem is, they also want to enjoy independence (something parents, in their roles as protectors, find hard to yield). Fortunately, there are some things both parents and young people can do to help the adolescent period of life be enjoyable, productive and God-honoring.

We can begin by applying biblical teaching. Go back to Proverbs 22:6. Let's look at the first two words, "train up." The Hebrew word for *train up* comes from the roof of the mouth or gums of the mouth. It is usually in two different forms. First, it speaks of breaking a wild stallion into submission by placing a bit in the horse's mouth and controlling that horse until his will is broken.

The second part of that word is used for the handmaiden or the midwife who helped in the delivery of a baby. The first thing she did when a baby was born was to crush a grape with her finger and put it into the mouth of that child. It created a sucking sensation and also a taste. When the words *train up* are put in this setting, they mean to bring your child into submission by creating a proper taste. Additionally, it means to create an atmosphere for your child that is conducive to his or her growth.

Notice that it says, "in the way he should go." It would be much easier if the Bible had said, "in the way the parent thinks he should go." But since it says, "in the way he should go," it means the child's way. A child who is properly trained is a child who has enjoyed a right environment and had proper training according to his gifts, characteristics, and mannerisms.

In Proverbs 30 there is an interesting passage: "There are [four] things. . .I do not understand: the way of an eagle in the sky, the way of a serpent on a rock, the way of a ship in the middle of the sea, and the way of a man with a maid," (vss. 18,19). The writer speaks of four distinct, unique characteristics and ways. He uses the same word found in the passage, "train up a child in the *way* he should go" (according to that child's gifts, that child's graces).

Now, we all know that we have children who are not alike in our homes. Isn't it amazing — same parents, same home, same environment, same dinner table, yet totally different children? In the beginning there was Cain and Abel, the first two children born. They were as different as night and day. The first two twins born, Jacob and Esau, were also totally different.

Now the Bible says in training up our children we should be sensitive to their characteristics and their mannerisms and train them up in the way they should go as individuals. In other words, regarding punishment and discipline, there is no standard right or wrong way to punish a child. We are to do our best to teach them according to their gifts and temperament.

When I was growing up, spanking didn't work with me. When I knew I was going to have a bad day, I put on five layers of underwear. I padded myself well. One time my brother put caps in his back pockets, and when Mom started spanking him, smoke began to roll out. She cracked up. No more spanking. For the next five years I constantly carried caps in my back pocket, just in case!

I always thought, give me that spanking and let me go on my way. But if I was told, "You're grounded for three days and can't go out and play with your friends," that was bad. I always made Mom regret that! Having me around the house for three days was more punishment for her than it was for me. As parents we need to be sensitive to the ways of our children. Less comparison to each other and more consideration to their individual personality will help in rearing them.

CHECK YOUR MOTIVES

In raising your children, ask yourself this questions, "Am I more concerned about my reputation than about my child's basic needs?" Boy, do I see that happen, especially in pastor's homes.

I used to go to camp and run around with other pastors' kids. Most of those PK's were sick and tired of being preacher's kids, and I used to wonder what was wrong with them. I was proud my father was a preacher. It beat being a bootlegger. Then I found out why they weren't proud. Their parents kept telling them not to do this and not to do that, because after all, "I'm a preacher and you've got to be good and look good around the laymen." My parents never told me that. They let me enjoy life. They loved me and taught me the Word. Sometimes I didn't always act very well, but that wasn't my fault — I just hung around with the laymen's kids too much!

We have to check our motives. Are we having children because we want some unfulfilled dream in our lives fulfilled through their lives? Are we putting undue pressure on them to fulfill it? We shouldn't.

DO NOT REJECT YOUR CHILD

Another thing we need to be careful of is rejecting our children. Yes, Christians do reject children — often in a passive, pouting way. When a parent withholds communication, affirmation or encouragement from a child, this is passive rejection. Many times I have had parents tell me their children have messed up their lives now that they are out of the house and are adults on their own. They ask, "Should I have them over to my home? I can't condone what they're doing." I say, "Absolutely, have them over to your home."

What is this that compels us to reject our children just because they are not behaving in the way we would like them to? There is a difference between disapproving of what they do and disapproving of them.

The beautiful example of this is in the story of the prodigal son. I don't think the father was overjoyed about the son who went out to sow his wild oats; but, the thing that thrills me about the waiting father is that the son came home and the father didn't say, "Son, you have sorely disappointed me. Look at all the sleepless nights you have put me through. Look at your older brother who stayed around the house being a good boy. How dare you act the way you did!" Instead, he said, "Welcome home, son."

Our passive rejection often is an attempt to control child behavior. Rejection is a powerful force, and it is always negative. It tears apart, separates, and wounds.

Acceptance is a positive thing. It draws together, unifies, knocks down barriers and heals wounds. Open up your heart to your child. Only the reassurance of an accepting, understanding love will lure the anxious, guilt-ridden child from behind his or her defenses. But acceptance is not always easy. It takes a determined and sometimes painful effort to hold our tongues and judgment and lovingly accept our children, sins and all. You may ask, "What is the biblical foundation for accepting our children?" It's Romans 5:8. "While we were yet sinners. . . ." We were involving ourselves in sin and being disobedient to God. "Christ died for us." He loved us when we were fit to be rejected.

RELINQUISH YOUR RIGHTS

I think it's terrible when parents hold onto their children when they should be out on their own. They think their children are solely for their personal enjoyment. They think, "After all, I clothed those kids, I changed their diapers. Now, they're doing this to me." Actually, there comes a time when parents absolutely must relinquish their control of their children.

Relinquish means:

1. To forsake "the right" to be proud. No parent has the right to demand their children fulfill their dreams.

2. To give up the right to uninterrupted enjoyment of your children. They were not created for this purpose. Possessiveness is damaging to both parent and child.

3. To cancel *all* debts. Your children owe you respect, nothing more. Don't blackmail them with stories of all you gave up so that they could prosper.

4. To allow your children to face problems. We must trust God with our children rather than trust our own ability to manage their lives forever.

Rather than try to dominate and control our children, we should try to be sensitive to their needs. Margaret, my wife, has such a sensitive spirit toward our children. She is always sensing and discerning. I am always missing and reacting. If there is one constant prayer of mine it is, "Oh, God, help me to be more sensitive to my children's unique needs." Paul Reese, a great preacher, accomplished many wonderful things in his life. Dr. Reese once was asked, "If there was anything in your life you would re-do, what would it be?" He replied, "I would go back to when my children were small and I would think, not through my mind's eye, but place myself where they are and think their thoughts."

I've tried to remember Paul's remark in dealing with my own children. It has helped me to avoid running into conflict areas that lead to pain on both sides.

Now, I realize that many of you already will have passed that point. You may be wondering how to cope with the pain you are already experiencing over wayward, disobedient, worldly children. The first thing I want to emphasize to you is that you should, under no circumstances, allow your embarrassment over your children's conduct to thwart you from carrying on your own church work involvement.

Often, our tendency, especially when our children aren't doing right, is to shy away from the church and the pastor. You know how it is. Our kids mess up on Saturday, but we come to church on Sunday and see the ideal families all around us. Makes you sick, doesn't it? The Jones girls, those cute twins, sing a duet. And the Smith's son announces he is going to college to become a medical missionary. Meanwhile, you don't even know where your kid is. So, you withdraw from the fellowship of believers. If there are any folks who should be loving us and encouraging us, praying for us, helping us through this process, it ought to be other Christians. They can help us shed the guilt we carry. (Refer back to chapter 8 for our discussion of coping with guilt.)

Most of the parental guilt we carry is false. If your guilt is real, ask God to forgive you. He forgives. Once He has forgiven you, try to leave it with Him. How many of you have had your faults and the things you did wrong with your children thrown up to you repeatedly? How many of you have thought more than once about something you did wrong with your kids?

Guilt is like a video recorder. I love to watch sports and video instant replays. In a championship game they have 26 instant replay cameras out there. After a good play happens, for the next two or three minutes they show you the replays. They not only show you how it looked on your television screen, but also how it was seen from seventeen different angles.

That's exactly what happens to people who carry guilt. Satan not only makes you remember what you did wrong with your kids in 1968, but he shows it to you from about seventeen different angles. If one wasn't bad enough, those instant replays continually come into your mind. One of the steps of healing is to be able to understand the difference between false guilt and real guilt. False guilt happens when we make no allowance for humanness. Real guilt is continual, known disobedience to God's principles.

Remember, we can only accept forgiveness as we give forgiveness to our children. "Forgive us our trespasses as we forgive those who trespass against us." God's forgiveness is complete. Yours toward your children must be, too.

You might say, "But you don't know how bad my kids are." In fact, you might be saying, "I don't even know where my kids are."

I'm going to quote from Psalm 139 in the Living Bible and substitute "my child" for the personal pronouns. Claim this Scripture for your children!

> "This is too glorious, too wonderful to believe! My child can never be lost to your Spirit. My child can never get away from my God. If my child goes up to heaven, you are there. If my child goes down to the place of the dead, you are there. If my child rides the morning winds to the farthest ocean, even there your hand will guide him, your strength will support him. If my child tries to hide in the darkness, the night becomes light around him. For even darkness cannot hide from God; to you the night shines as bright as day. Darkness and light are both alike to you. . . .How precious it is, Lord, to realize that you are thinking about my child constantly. He can't even count how many times a day your thoughts turn toward him. And when my child wakens in the morning, you are still thinking of him" (from vss. 6-12,17,18).

Do you remember the TV commercial that used to be more common than it is today? It came on the news, a little blurb that asked, "Parents, do you know where your children are?" Hopefully, you do. But I've got good news for you: if you don't know where they are, I know someone who does. I know someone who knows right where they are physically, spiritually, emotionally. We all know that someone has the ability to reach them, touch them, love them, and bring them back to Himself.

Let's be like the waiting father looking for the return of his prodigal son. He had patience while his son was gone. He also had forgiveness when he came home.

CHAPTER 13

Can
My Faith
be Increased?

In Hebrews chapter 11 the writer explains the value of faith. He demonstrates it through example and illustrations. In verse 1 we have the definition or description of faith. "Faith is the assurance of things hoped for, the conviction of things not seen." In verse 2 the writer tells us that it was by faith that men of old gained approval.

It was by faith that the great men of the Old Testament gained approval from God. In verse 3 the writer says, "By faith we understand that the world was prepared by the Word of God, so that what is seen was not made out of things which are visible." It is by faith that we understand what the world tries to explain and never can. We have answers from God.

In verse 4, by faith Abel offered to God a sacrifice through which he obtained God's testimony that he was righteous. God testified about Abel's gifts. Wouldn't it be beautiful for God to testify concerning our gifts, and for God to testify concerning our righteousness? As Abel, by faith, offered a sacrifice, he received assurance from God.

Enoch was taken up to the presence of God because of his faith. He did not see death and was not found because God took him up.

It was obvious that faith is a great benefit to the believer in his or her walk with God. It gives approval, answers, assurance and access to God. Paul, in Romans 1:16, talks about the gospel. In this presentation to the church he says he is not ashamed of the gospel. The reason for his lack of shame is that "it is the power of God for salvation to everyone who believes, to the Jew first and also the Greek. For in it the righteousness of God is revealed from faith to faith; as it is written, 'But the righteous man shall live by faith.'"

Let's look at the phrase "faith to faith." The question is, "How do I receive more faith?" The answer is here. The first word "faith" speaks of a primary faith. That is the foundation in which every person who loves the Lord Jesus Christ builds his life. The first faith is saving faith. The second faith is power-giving faith, the faith of fruitfulness. Faith is two-dimensional. One faith we build upon, the other identifies us.

The first word "faith" implies the faith that saves. It gives us eternal life. The second word "faith" is the faith that sustains. It gives us daily life. It is our walk, hour by hour, day by day. The first "faith" is the faith of assurance; it tells us we are God's children, and it tells us that we are secure in God; the second "faith" deals with our capacity, and tells us what we can become. It gives us the confidence to expand and stretch. The first faith is a faith that redeems; it gives us security. The second faith is the faith that risks.

The apostle Paul, when writing to the church at Rome, said that through the righteousness of God we can go from faith to faith. The first faith is a gift that brings righteousness to us. The second faith is the growth that follows that righteousness.

Let me share a couple of other translations. The New English Bible says "The righteousness of God starts in faith and ends in faith." Phillips says it is a "process begun and continued by their faith." Williams comes the closest to the original language, "The way of faith that leads to a greater faith."

Paul says it is essential that we have a primary salvation faith. It is not of works; it is always by faith. It is a gift; the gift of God to have faith in Jesus Christ as our personal Savior. Once we have that primary faith, it is then important for us to expand into a greater dimension, more powerful faith. We are made right by faith that we might live rightly by faith. A paraphrase of this is: The righteousness of God is formed *out of faith* and has a goal of higher faith.

Let's examine that primary faith for just a moment. Our faith is only as good as its object. Faith is not valid simply because it is intense. That's a description of fanaticism. A fanatic is a person who has incredible faith, but the object of his faith may not be valid. Faith is only as valid as the faithfulness of the object. Therefore, faith to be what it could be or should be must be directed toward an object. The Christian's faith is in Jesus. "The just shall live by faith." Not just any kind of faith, but faith in the atonement of our Lord Jesus Christ. Faith in the fact that He died for the world. Faith that we need not perish, but that can have everlasting life. That is faith we can rely upon. It has an object. Valid faith has an object. It is not what the Sunday school kid thought when he said, "Faith is believing something you know isn't true."

If you loan someone fifty dollars and he takes off, you can have all the faith in the world that you're going to get that money back. You can get up every day and say, "I know today my friend will bring back my fifty dollars." But if that person is not reliable, you can have all the faith in the world and never receive that fifty dollars back.

I've seen missionary slides and films about a father who brought his sick child to a witch doctor who administered a potion and performed a dance, yet the child died. The reason was not because the father didn't have faith. The man probably had incredible faith, the faith literally to risk his child's life. However, the object was not valid.

If you want to increase your faith, you must put your faith in Jesus. You must have a primary, valid faith before you can have a powerful faith. You must have a right and solid foundation. Jesus is the one. Paul said that the moment you trust Jesus as Savior, you can go on to a greater faith, a higher faith, an expansive faith, a more powerful faith!

SPECIFIC WAYS TO HAVE A MORE POWERFUL FAITH

Once you accept Christ as your personal Savior and thus have created a primary faith as the foundation of your life, you'll be ready to enhance the power of your faith.

1. You can begin by understanding that your faith can grow. Faith has degrees. Sometimes in my counseling I run into people who feel they do not have the faith they desire because they cannot measure up to other Christians who evidence overwhelming faith.

The good news is that if you have primary faith in Jesus Christ, your faith is expandable and you can grow. Remember when Jesus was in the boat and they awakened Him because they were frightened and wanted Him to calm the sea? He looked at them and said, "O ye of *little faith*" (KJV). They had faith, but just a little bit of it. Remember the lady whose daughter was possessed and she came and asked Jesus to touch her? As she continually persisted, Jesus finally looked at her and said, "Your faith is great." Remember when Paul wrote to the church at Thessalonica? He said he was thankful "because your faith is greatly enlarged, and the love of each one of you toward one another grows ever greater" (2 Thess. 1:3).

Our faith is like our biceps; we have them but we must work them and keep them exercised to keep them strong. We must exercise our faith to become effective and useful in life. We all have the seed of faith in ourselves. We all have the potential for growth. If our faith is to expand as God wants it to expand, the first thing we must accept is the fact that it is possible for our faith to be greater tomorrow than it is today.

2. Your faith will begin to grow in your life when you associate with people who also have tremendous faith. In Romans 1:12 Paul deals with this truth. He said, "I may be encouraged together with you while among you, each of us by the other's faith, both yours and mine." In other words, Paul is saying he would love to be with them because he could encourage their faith and they could encourage his. In 2 Corinthians 10:15 Paul wrote, "As your faith grows, we shall be. . .enlarged even more by you." Your faith as it grows will help others' faith to grow.

In 1 Thessalonians 3:2 Paul wrote, "And we sent Timothy, our brother and God's fellow worker in the gospel of Christ, to strengthen and encourage you as to your faith." So, it's possible for our faith to grow by associating with the right people. My words of encouragement to you are to find a friend who has great faith!

In my observation of people and their Christian walk, I have found it is not their circumstances that cause their problems. It is not their situations that cause their doubts or their questioning, so much as it is the crowd they associate with. I have found that good circumstances and bad friends equal problems. Bad circumstances and good friends equal victory.

The people with whom you associate can either weigh you down or lift you up. Let me explain it this way. You wake up in the morning with a splitting headache. You don't know whether to reach for Alka-Seltzer, Pepto-Bismol or Tylenol. So you get up and all three are gone. What's the first thing you do? You fall on your knees and pray a prayer like this: "Oh, God, it's going to be a bad day. Don't let me see so-and-so." Or you pray a prayer like this: "Oh, God, it's going to be a bad day. Let me see so-and-so." Isn't it true that when you're down there are some people you really want to see and there are other people you will go to incredible lengths to avoid?

I'll tell you the difference. One is a friend of fear and the other is a friend of faith. One will show you problems and the other will show you Jesus. And if you get around the one who shows you Jesus, after prayer and maybe a few Scripture readings, you will feel better, be encouraged, see that the problem is not insurmountable, get a spring in your step and a smile on your face and say, "With God's help and the faith of a friend, I can make it." But if you spend about five minutes with a friend of fear and he or she talks to you about the problems you have as well as seventeen others you hadn't thought of, you become depressed. After the conversation has ended the only good thing about talking to that person is that you realize that before you talked to them it wasn't nearly as bad as you thought. Find a friend of faith.

3. Read and embrace God's Word. Paul challenged Timothy in 1 Timothy 4:6 to be constantly nourished on the words of the faith. In Acts 16:5 when the early church was growing and the apostles were going from town to town teaching the Word, the churches were "being strengthened in the faith." First John 5:13 tells us, "These things I have written to you who believe in the name of the Son of God, in order that you may know that you have eternal life." These words were written to help you come to the knowledge that your sins are forgiven.

The life of D. L. Moody has been a constant encouragement to me. One time he said, "I prayed for faith and thought that some day faith would come down and strike me like lightning. But faith did not seem to come. One day I read in the tenth chapter of Romans, 'Faith cometh by hearing and hearing by the

Word of God.' I had (up to this time) closed my Bible and prayed for faith. I now opened my Bible and began to study, and faith has been growing ever since."

4. Practice prayer and fasting. Remember the man (Matthew 17) who came to the disciples and asked for help for his mentally ill son? He asked the disciples to pray for the boy. They prayed and nothing happened. Then Jesus prayed and something did happen. The disciples all became discouraged and said, "Lord, why is it when we prayed for him nothing happened?" The Lord said in Matthew 17:20, "Because of the littleness of your faith." Then He talked about faith being as a mustard seed. It is very small but has wonderful growth potential. As faith develops, Christians can say to the mountain, "'Move from here to there,' and it shall move." Jesus said, "But this kind does not go out except by prayer and fasting." There are some areas of our lives in which we will never have the faith we need until we become totally immersed in prayer and fasting, believing God to give that for which we pray.

5. Remember past victories. Hebrews 10:32 says, "But remember the former days, when, after being enlightened, you endured a great conflict of sufferings." One way to "remember the former days" is to keep a victory diary. It is a prayer record book where you can go back and see when you asked God for something, when you prayed for it, and when God answered your prayer. It will encourage you in times when you have a big project in front of you.

David found that remembering his past success with God increased his faith for greater challenge. In 1 Samuel 17 David came down to the army camp to bring food to his brothers. Goliath was on the other side, challenging Israel. No one would pick up the challenge so David said he would fight Goliath. Most of the people in the army thought David was a little crazy. "When the words which David spoke were heard, they told them to Saul, and he sent for him. And David said to Saul, 'Let no man's heart fail on account of him; your servant will go and fight with this Philistine'" (vss. 31,32). David just came to Saul and told him not to get shaken. Saul said to David in verse 33, "You are not able to go against this Philistine to fight with him; for you are but a youth while he has been a warrior from his youth." David was ready to go to battle but the king said he couldn't do that.

In verse 34 David said to Saul, "Your servant was tending his father's sheep. When a lion or a bear came and took a lamb from the flock, I went out after him and attacked him, and rescued it from his mouth; and when he rose up against me, I seized him by his beard and struck him and killed him. Your servant has killed the lion and the bear; and this uncircumcised Philistine will be like one of them, since he has taunted the armies of the living God." And David said, "The Lord who delivered me from the paw of the lion and from the paw of the bear, He will deliver me from the hand of this Philistine." David knew that if God could help him fight against a bear and against a lion, then God could help him fight against Goliath. He remembered his past. He remembered what faith had done previously for him.

Let me tell you what the world's system will try to do to your faith. Saul saw that David was determined to go out and fight Goliath, and look what happened: "Then Saul clothed David with his garments and put a bronze helmet on his head, and he clothed him with armor. And David girded his sword over his armor and *tried to walk.*"

David was supposed to go out and fight, but with King Saul's armor on, poor little David couldn't even crawl to Goliath! Why? The world, as soon as it sees your faith, will try to put its system on you and bring that system into your life of faith. The world will try to put its weight on you. David saw that it would not work. He saw that his success would come from his faith in God, not from Saul's armor. Blessed is the man or woman who can understand that faith in God is greater than all the armor of the world. "If God be for us, who can be against us?"

David said, "I cannot go with these, for I have not tested them." David took them off. "And he took his stick in his hand and chose for himself five smooth stones from the brook, and put them in the shepherd's bag which he had, even in his pouch, and his sling was in his hand; and he approached the Philistine." David was armed with faith. It had grown and developed over the years. Now, it was mature.

An active faith is a growing faith. We started off in Hebrews 11, "Now faith *is* the assurance. . . ." Little words are so descriptive. In giving the definition of faith the Hebrew writer did not say "then faith *was.*" You can take off that little word "now" and still have a beautiful definition of faith. "Faith *is* the substance of things hoped for, the evidence of things not seen" (KJV). Why did the Hebrew writer under the inspiration of God's spirit put the word *now* in there? Because he wanted to teach us that faith is to be expansive, growing, active right now. People who have a faith that is growing are people whose faith is active.

In my first church, a wonderful lady was saved and became involved in lay ministry. Because of financial pressures she had to go to work. Slowly, she had to lay aside some of the gifts and ministries God had given her until, at best, she would show up twice a month to occupy a pew. I never will forget the panic on her face when one day she walked into the office and said, "Pastor, I have lost my faith." She didn't mean she had lost her primary faith. She meant she had lost her powerful faith. She had lost the faith that really made the difference in her walk with God. It was that daily, sustaining walk that this faith brings. Why had she lost it? Because she ceased to be active.

We've learned two things. We've learned that faith is primary. It has to have an object and that object is Jesus Christ. If we do not know Christ as personal Savior, there's no need for us to think about a secondary faith. Jesus is who you and I need first. Give your life to Him and then go on to the secondary faith.

We've also learned that when you've made that relationship with Christ what it should be, you then can go on to a powerful faith. This is a faith that makes us more than conquerors through Him.

My four-year-old son, Joel Porter, has always been a little bit afraid of water. My wife and I were talking about this fear and we decided to get Joel some "swimmies" that you place under your arms to hold you above the water. After much encouragement Joel went into the water. In the beginning he was not sure the swimmies would hold him up. But the moment he realized that as long as he had the swimmies on he could go all over the pool, he became a fish. We could hardly get him out of the pool! Within a couple days he would even jump into the water.

One night I said, "Joel, you don't need those swimmies. I've been watching you, and you kick your feet well and you paddle your arms like you're supposed to. You can do it."

He looked at me and said, "Can I?"

I suggested that he take off his swimmies, and he did. He walked to the side of the pool, and I encouraged him to jump in. He said, "Will you come into the water, Daddy?"

I said yes and went to the place in the water where Joel pointed. I was now close enough so that when he jumped in I would be there.

He asked, "Will you catch me?"

I said, "No. But I'll be beside you, and if you need me, I'll pick you up."

He jumped in and started dog paddling. I stayed right beside him for encouragement, but I never touched him. In a few moments he paddled to the side of the pool. Then we did what we do so well at our house — we had celebration time. I stood him beside the pool and lifted his arms up and called him a champion swimmer. All the family — Elizabeth, Margaret, and I — clapped and gave him a standing ovation.

I said, "Joel, you can do that again."

He got back out and told me to stand in the same place again. "Will you catch me?"

"No, but I'll be beside you, if you need me." He did that four times.

That night Joel went to bed absolutely exhausted. His favorite statement was, "I'm proud of me." You see, he didn't need me to help him, he just needed to know I was there when he needed me.

God looks at us as we jump into the pool of life, and He gives us projects that are big to us. Basically we say, "God, I'll jump in but will you catch me?"

"No, But I'll be beside you," God says. "And if you run out of steam, My grace is sufficient. I'll just take you into My everlasting loving arms. Since you trusted Me by faith to jump, you can trust Me in My faithfulness to pick you up."

So, we jump into the pool of life and paddle furiously. God walks beside us and we begin to reach destinations that we previously felt were impossible. Exhausted, we hold on to the side of the pool with a smile on our face. We have just increased our faith!

CHAPTER 14

Why Are
My Prayers
Sometimes Not Answered?

Many times people ask me, "Pastor, why is it that I cannot seem to get my prayers through to God?"

Let's consider first the obvious. Many times people never receive an answer from God because they have not prayed. The Word teaches us that we "have not because we ask not." Jesus re-emphasized this when He spoke to His followers one time, "Until now you have asked for nothing my My name; ask and you will receive." It is possible for us in our Christian walk to assume certain privileges or answers without prayer.

UNCONFESSED SIN

There are several problem areas that I want to point out to you that prevent us from hearing God in our prayer life. One of the most detrimental factors is unconfessed sin. When we are fully aware that we are acting in sin yet we refuse to confess it, we permit it to form a barrier between ourselves and God.

In Psalm 66:18 the psalmist said, "If I regard wickedness in my heart, the Lord will not hear." That word *regard* could be substituted by many words. If I cherish sin in my heart, the Lord will not hear me. If I tolerate sin in my life. If I foster it. The writer gives us a picture of a person who is knowingly sinning against God and seemingly does not have any sense of urgency to get rid of that sin. He is caught up in it, accepting it, perhaps even enjoying it in his life. So, the psalmist said that since he is living with that unconfessed sin in his life, the Lord Himself will not hear him.

Isaiah 59:1,2 is a very clear passage that informs us that God is able to answer our prayers but sometimes chooses not to. "Behold the Lord's hand is not so short that it cannot save; neither is His ear so dull that it cannot hear. *But* your iniquities have made a separation between you and your God, and your sins have hidden His face from you, so that He does not hear." The Bible very clearly tells us that sin separates us from God so that He will not hear or answer our prayers. Again, I reemphasize that this is the tolerated, accepted and known sin in our lives.

The principle is this: Before I pray for a change in my circumstances, I should pray for a change in my character. Before I ask God to rearrange my life, I should ask God to rearrange me. All successful prayer begins with confession of any known sin in our lives. The moment that we confess our sin, the channel is opened up and God can begin to work through us. James teaches us in chapter 5, verse 16, "The earnest prayer of a righteous man (a man who has been made right by the cleansing action and confession of his sins) has great power and wonderful results" (TLB). We must clear up the channel by confessing our sin.

Norman Vincent Peale tells a story from his childhood. He found a cigar and went to the alley to light it. He didn't like what he was tasting at all but he had the sense of feeling "important." As he puffed away, his dad happened to come along. He saw his dad and immediately put the cigar behind his back and tried to carry on a normal conversation. To divert his father's attention, he pointed out a billboard that announced a circus coming to town. He said, "Dad, can I go to the circus?" As he pleaded with his father, his dad said, "Norman, you need to learn something in life. You don't ask requests when you have smoldering disobedience behind your back."

Have you ever tried to divert God's attention? You're really trying to get through to Him on a request and God is trying to deal with the smoldering disobedience in your life. You will talk to Him about the circus coming to town but He wants you to discuss that unconfessed, realized sin that causes problems in your prayer life.

UNFORGIVING SPIRIT

Another barrier to a successful prayer life is an unforgiving spirit. Have you ever noticed in the Gospels how many times Jesus connects forgiveness with answered prayer? Remember in Matthew 18 when Peter came to Jesus and asked how many times he should forgive another person? He was big in his estimates. He asked if he should forgive seven times; that's more than twice what the Hebrew law required. Peter was being very generous. We know what the Lord answered. Jesus said, "Seventy times seven." That is 490 times for the very same sin. You see, Jesus is trying to teach Peter that forgiveness is not a matter of mathematics. Forgiveness is not an act but an attitude. It is not a spurt but a spirit. It is a lifestyle. It's a way I am to act toward my brothers and sisters.

In Matthew 5:23,24 Jesus talks about coming to the altar. He says that if we begin to pray and talk to God and we realize that we have something wrong between ourselves and another, we should leave the altar and go and restore that broken relationship, then come back and bring gifts to the altar. You see, when you have a forgiving spirit it not only makes your prayer life more effective, it makes your heart lighter. When the heart is right, the heart is light. It makes you more effective in your daily walk.

Our relationship with others must be right before our relationship with God can be right. It's impossible for you to have an effective prayer life if you are carrying a grudge or licking old wounds.

UNSURRENDERED WILL

James 4:3 says, "You ask and do not receive, because you ask with wrong motives." Why is it that we pray? If our motives are wrong, many times the answers will not come. I have seen people, very genuine in their prayer lives, who have had motives that were not quite as pure as they should be. I have known wives of unsaved husbands who probably, if they were honest, were concerned for the salvation of their husbands so their lives would be easier at home. I think that is a legitimate request, but probably the motive is not as pure as just praying for the husband's salvation because of what Christ needs to do in that life.

This becomes a little more difficult when we engage ourselves in intercessory prayer because we're dealing with two wills, our own and the one belonging to the other person.

In praying for some great cause like world peace, the wills of millions of people enter into the picture. Even though your will is fully yielded to God's desire that all people should find salvation (2 Peter 3:9), an unsurrendered will on the part of the person (or persons) for whom you are praying can neutralize your prayer and cause it to go unanswered.

To pray "in Jesus' name" is to say in substance, "Lord, this is how it looks to me. From my limited point of view I think it ought to come out this way. But I do not know everything. If part of my prayer is wrong, then hear and answer only that part of it which is right — that part which is in keeping with Your spirit and Your name." To pray "in Jesus' name" is to pray with one eye open. It is to keep one eye focused on your prayer itself — examining it, measuring it, weighing it to make certain that what you ask is in keeping with the character of the one in whose name you ask it. To pray "in Jesus' name" is to stop giving orders. It is to turn command and authority over to Him. It is to accept the simple fact that the purpose of prayer is not to change life to suit you, but to change yourself to suit life.

Psalm 33:13 is an interesting verse. "The Lord looks from heaven; He sees *all* the sons of men." God sees me, but He also sees the crowd. He will not do anything to benefit one person if it will be a detriment to many. Sometimes our prayer life is not effective because we pray selfishly with only our own needs in mind.

When I was a kid growing up in Ohio, there were many summer storms, and too many times rainy days messed up this kid's plans. I always looked forward to the annual Sunday school picnic for our church. I asked God not to let it rain on that day. I was very sincere because that was a big day for me. One year in particular we were in a drought of six weeks and the farmers in Ohio were suffering. But I prayed, "Oh, God, don't let it rain!" I remember it poured all day. I was crushed. Why didn't God answer my prayer? God didn't answer my prayer because He had the needs of the state of Ohio in mind over a baseball game at a Sunday school picnic.

A lot of time we, as adults, have that same disregard for others. We want to satisfy our own needs. Thankfully, God sees the whole and judges on total need. The crowd is more in need than the individual. Romans 8:28 says, "God causes all things to work together for good to those who love God." It gives us the picture that the individual is just a part of the whole and all things work *together* for good. Perhaps it may not be good for the individual but good for the whole.

GOD IS SOVEREIGN

Our prayers are also ineffective when we do not understand that God is sovereign. The principle is this: if all our prayers were answered, you (not God) would be in control. You may be thinking, that doesn't sound like a bad idea. There may be things you'd really like to control. If you could just have the world in your hands for one day you could cure all the ills of society. But the longer we think about it, the more the responsibility begins to weigh heavily on our shoulders. Sometimes we disregard God's ways that are higher than our ways. God is in control of all things. He is not some kind of puppet whose strings can be pulled in response to our whims and whimpers.

Sometimes we are like the Scottish woman who traveled around Scotland selling her wares in small country towns. When she came to a fork in the road she would throw up a stick in the air and whichever way the stick fell she would follow that leading. That stick became good luck to her. One day the townspeople saw her do that and the stick fell and she picked it up again. It fell the same way and she picked it up and threw it again. It finally fell a different way and that is the way she traveled. They asked, "Why did you do it three times?" And she answered, "The first two times the stick pointed to a way I didn't want to go." We do that, don't we? "Now, God, I've given You five chances; here's a sixth one. I'll keep reminding You until we get this right." We totally bypass the sovereignty of God. It hampers effective prayer.

WHERE'S YOUR FAITH?

James 1:5-7 says, "But if any of you lacks wisdom, let him ask of God, who gives to all men generously and without reproach, and it will be given to him. But let him ask in faith without any doubting for the one who doubts is like the surf of the sea driven and tossed by the wind. For let not that man expect that he will receive anything from the Lord."

For many years scientists wanted to harness the sea. If they could somehow harness all that power, we'd have all the electricity we'd ever need. But the waves of the sea are undependable. They go one way and then another way. Sometimes they even remain calm. Perhaps James spoke of the Sea of Galilee, known for its unpredictability. One moment it can be calm and the next minute turbulent. He tells us that when our faith is like that, reaching a high peak and then a low ebb, our prayer lives will not be effective.

When we look in the Gospels, we see that faith and forgiveness probably affect our prayer lives more than any other thing. Those words appear throughout the four Gospels. In Matthew 9:29 Jesus said, "Be it done to you according to your faith." In Matthew 17:20 we read, "If you have faith as a mustard seed. . .nothing shall be impossible to you." In Luke 7:50 it says, "Your faith has saved you; go in peace." Matthew 21:21 says, "If you have faith, and do not doubt. . .it shall happen." Five different times it is recorded in the Gospels that Jesus said, "Your faith has made you whole." So important is faith in our prayer lives that Jesus looked at Peter one day and told him, "I have prayed for you, that your faith may not fail." The principle is this: To make my prayer a force instead of a farce I must hunt for the question marks in my life. I must ask myself what it is that makes me lack the faith I need to grab hold of the horns of the altar.

We must be like the man who came to Jesus on behalf of his son saying, "I do believe; help my unbelief." May God give us the ability to grapple with the areas in our lives that are not reaching out and touching God by faith.

COMMITMENT TO PRAYER

Do you pray the way you bob for apples? You stick your head down and try to bring out the apple in your mouth. You don't keep you head down long however. You're in and out, up and down. You're never consistent or persistent. I don't mean praying long and loud prayers. I don't want you to be like the man who prayed so loud that it caused a little girl to look at her dad and ask, "If he lived closer to God would he have to pray as loud as he does?"

I'm referring to a persistency with sincerity; a commitment to believing that prayer is a way of life and without it we will never be the Christians we should be. Again I refer to the type of prayer James mentions: the effectual, fervent prayer of a righteous man that avails much. Or as Weymouth says, "Powerful is the heart-felt supplicaton of a righteous man." Or as Phillips says, "Tremendous power is made available through a good man's earnest prayer." Williams says, "An upright man's prayer, when it is at work, is extremely powerful."

It is not the geometry of your prayers — how long they are; it is not the arithmetic of your prayers — how many they are; it is not the wording of your prayers — how beautiful they are; it is not the volume of your prayers — how loud they are. Always, it's the intensity of your prayers.

In Korea I saw a commitment to prayer like I've seen nowhere else. Korean Christians really know how to stay strong in prayer. Almost every church there has a Prayer Mountain. Prayer chapels are built right into a mountain and have little doors. On the outside you'll see little shoes. The people take their shoes off and go inside. Some will enter with just water for forty days of fasting and prayer. When I realize that the average Korean Christian spends his vacation time in prayer in one of those little rooms in Prayer Mountain, I am overwhelmed.

"Prayer," said Charles Haddon Spurgeon, "is like a rope on a bell. When tugged, the great bell rings in the ears of God. Some scarcely stir the bell; others give but an occasional pinch at the rope. But he who wins with heaven is the man who grasps the rope boldly and pulls continually with all his might."

Jesus tells us, "Ask, seek, and knock." Those are not past tense words. It is not ask once and it shall be given to you. They are present tense words. It means ask now and keep asking. Keep on seeking. Keep on knocking. Our prayer life then becomes effective. The reason for that is because it takes time for prayer to change us. God's objective in prayer is not to change His mind, but to change ours. Sometimes that takes lots of time. Persistency in prayer clarifies our thinking and purifies our motives. It's something we all need.

PUTTING FEET TO PRAYERS

Sometimes we do not have our prayers answered because we expect our prayers to do everything for us. I love the story about the Catholic priest and his friend who went to a boxing match. One boxer entered the ring and crossed himself. The friend looked at the Catholic priest and said, "Is that going to help that guy?" The priest looked back with a twinkle in his eye and said, "It will if he's a good fighter."

Sometimes people pray as if they expected God to do absolutely everything for them while they did nothing. James talks about that, doesn't he? In James 2:14 we read, "What use is it, my brethren, if a man says he has faith, but he has no works? Can that faith save him?" Then he gives an example, "If a brother or sister is without clothing and in need of daily food, and one of you says to them, 'Go in peace, be warmed and be filled,' and yet you do not give them what is necessary for their body, what use is that? Even so faith, if it has no works, is dead, being by itself."

He means it's not enough to pray that a person would be warm with their clothing. We need to give them something. We need to put action to our prayers. The principle is: My great need is not faith and works, but faith that works.

THE PRAYER BEHIND THE PRAYER

We need to balance our prayers with works. Just as we should not pray without working, we should not try to work out all of our problems without relying on prayer. Isaiah 55:8,9 says, "'My thoughts are not your thoughts, neither are your ways My ways,' declares the Lord. 'For as the heavens are higher than the earth, so are My ways higher than your ways, and My thoughts higher than your thoughts." Sometimes we need to understand God's plan, or God's way, in our prayer life.

St. Augustine, one of the great fathers of the early church, had a praying mother by the name of Monica. When Augustine was growing up he was anything but a saint. In his teenage years, he was a playboy. His mother used to pray that God would take hold of him. One day he told his mother he was going to Rome to live. His mother's heart sank because she knew Rome was a wicked city. If he went there he wouldn't be under her influence any longer.

Monica prayed, "God, don't allow him to go to Rome." But Augustine went. While he was in Rome, he came under the influence of Ambrose, Bishop of Rome. Through that influence, he was brought into salvation and became one of the great early church fathers.

What I want you to see is this: Monica's prayer was, "God, don't let my son go to Rome. It is wicked." But that wasn't really her prayer. Her prayer was, "God, save my son." When St. Augustine went to Rome she panicked and felt that would make the problem worse. She didn't understand God's sovereign plan. God had to bring the boy to Rome to get him under the influence of Ambrose. How many times do we pray as if we had the plans all laid out for God? God smiles. We are so naive.

God is more interested in answering the spirit of my prayer than the letter of it. Florence Nightingale, that remarkable woman who was years ahead of her time in many ways, asked the practical question: "What is the use of praying to be delivered from 'plague and pestilence' so long as the common sewers are allowed to flow into the river? If God sends a visitation of cholera, which is the more preferable reading of His mind — that He sent it in order that men might pray to Him for relief from it, or in order that they should, themselves, be driven to remove the predisposing causes?"

Ponder the story of Moses, who repeatedly prayed he might enter into the Promised Land, but whose petition was not granted. Here was a giant among men, a stalwart of the Lord, a leader of the people. Yet the one thing for which he repeatedly prayed was denied him. Why? Because this man who stood for God in the midst of the people had on one occasion been exceedingly ungodly. In a moment of anger and impatience he had smitten a rock in disobedience to God. The false image of God which that act gave to an immature people had to be erased. Somehow they needed to know that this picture of God with flashing eyes and flailing fist was distorted. More importantly, they needed to learn that no man — even a leader — can sin and get away with it.

Moses had dishonored God. For the sake of the people, he had to be punished. So, God, in effect, said to him: "Moses, you will not go into Canaan. You may lead the people up to the border. You may even see inside. But you cannot go in." People cannot be above the law. No one is exempt from obedience to God's plan.

How Moses prayed for a reprieve! How he earnestly petitioned God for a reversal of this decision; not once, but over and over he asked until God finally said, "Speak to Me no more on this matter" (Deuteronomy 3:36). I believe that if only Moses had been involved, God would have granted his request. God loved him. But there were others to be considered. They had to be taught the necessity of obedience in a way they would never forget. So, his petition was denied in order that the larger purpose might be served.

Ever since then, Hebrew and Christian mothers have taken their children into their arms and have told them the story of Moses — the man of God who could not go into the Promised Land because he was disobedient. Through the telling of that tale, both young

and old have had this great fact nailed down for them: Disobedience
can be forgiven, but the consequences must still be lived with.

If Moses could speak to us now, I believe he would say he
was glad his prayer was denied. Deeper, wider, and higher than
any concern for personal achievement was Moses' desire to lead
the people into full possession of all God had promised them.
This was the prayer behind his prayer. When his superficial desire
was denied, his real request was answered. He was given a no
which turned out to be yes, and, thus, a larger purpose was served.

Consider, too, the experience of Paul. Three times Paul prayed
that he might be relieved from a "thorn in the flesh." So far as
we know, he never was. He carried this malady (eye trouble,
epilepsy, allergy, recurrent attacks of malaria?) with him to the
grave. But did Paul pray in vain? Not at all. Though God denied
the petition, he answered the man. He said to Paul: "My grace is
sufficient for you" (2 Corinthians 12:9). Through this grace of
God, Paul learned to triumph in suffering. He entered into a
relationship with the Father that few men have shared. With the
pain came the presence of Jesus and the persuasion that "The
sufferings of this present time are not worthy to be compared with
the glory that is to be revealed to us" (Romans 8:18).

For Paul that gift was quite enough. Although his petition (that
he might be relieved from the thorn in the flesh) was denied, the
petition behind his petition, the longing behind his longing, the
desire behind his desire (to know Jesus and the power of His
resurrection) was granted. And Paul lived to speak lovingly of the
day when no was really yes.

One last scene completes the picture, and here we truly tread
on holy ground. A figure kneels in the Garden of Gethsemane.
Below Him is the brook of Kidron. Behind Him stands a grove
of gnarled olive trees. Above Him is a rotund moon whose brightness
makes the shadowy rocks all the more foreboding. As He kneels
there, this one who knew no sin struggles with the indescribable
horror of taking on Himself the sin of the world: "My Father, if
it is possible, let this cup pass from Me" (Matthew 26:39). There
is desperate urgency in His words. "If there is any other way — if
there is any other alternative — if there is any other means whereby
the salvation of the world can be secured, let this cup pass." But
the cup did not pass. Why not? So the prayer behind His prayer
(that all might be saved) could be answered. Through a momentary
denial of the letter of Jesus' prayer, there came the eternal answer

to the spirit of His prayer. The real purpose for which He had come was fulfilled.

So it often is with us. When we think that God is not listening, or saying no to our prayers, in truth He actually is preparing a better *yes* answer for us.

CHAPTER 15

How Can I Glorify God In My Job?

Before reading this chapter, please complete the following quiz. Read the questions and circle the number that most clearly describes your present job situation.

1. Does my work ever compete with Jesus for first place in my life?

   Always 1 2 3 4 5 6 7 8 9 10 Never

2. Have I neglected the essential relationships of life among family or friends because of my work?

   Always 1 2 3 4 5 6 7 8 9 10 Never

3. Am I tempted to compromise my beliefs in order to give in or keep a position?

   Always 1 2 3 4 5 6 7 8 9 10 Never

4. Do I overwork as an escape from greater responsibilities?

   Always 1 2 3 4 5 6 7 8 9 10 Never

5. Is my job one in which I can glorify Jesus Christ?

Never 1 2 3 4 5 6 7 8 9 10 Always

6. Do I give God at least 10 percent of the earnings from my job?

Never 1 2 3 4 5 6 7 8 9 10 Always

7. Do I live a wholesome life — a combination of work and recreation, enrichment and personal growth?

Never 1 2 3 4 5 6 7 8 9 10 Always

8. Do the people with whom I work know that I am a Christian?

Never 1 2 3 4 5 6 7 8 9 10 Always

9. Am I an attractive Christian, someone others want to know because Christ is in my life?

Never 1 2 3 4 5 6 7 8 9 10 Always

10. Does my employer receive from me honesty and a willingness to work faithfully for my wages?

Never 1 2 3 4 5 6 7 8 9 10 Always

11. Have I claimed my place of employment for the Lord? Am I a communicator of grace in that place?

Never 1 2 3 4 5 6 7 8 9 10 Always

Instructions: Add up the numbers circled from the eleven questions and categorize with this key:

0-33   "It's me, it's me, O Lord, standing in the need of prayer."

34-66   "Lord Jesus, I long to be perfectly whole."

67-100   "It is well with my soul."

101-110 "I'll fly away."

In this, our final chapter, I hope to provide some tangible helps by which you can take the material learned in the previous chapters and put it to use not only where you live but also where you work. In attempting to discover how you can glorify God in the job you perform, we would do well to begin with the basics of how God views work.

Paul said that whether you eat or drink or whatever you do, it should be done for the glory of God. That's a tall order. We'll need parameters to help us in this. Let's keep it simple. There are four words we can use as guides.

1. *Prominence*

Prominence is the awareness of God's presence. Whenever God's glory came down upon His people, biblically and historically there was an awareness that God was present. The Shekina glory of God was said to have descended on His people.

Today, we have the indwelling Holy Spirit which accomplishes the same thing. It should be obvious. Paul said that we glorify God when people with whom we work are aware of the Christ whom we serve. They see Him in us. In an ungodly, unwholesome atmosphere there should be a distinct difference in our lives. It should be an elevating example to others around us. Until they begin to see God in us, there will be no desire for them to know Christ personally.

In Acts 4:13 when the people looked at Peter and John and saw that they were untrained men, yet they were able to preach, teach, and speak foreign languages, they came to the conclusion that Peter and John obviously *must* have been with Jesus. It is impossible for us to spend much time with God and not reflect Him in our lives.

2. *Purpose*

God has a purpose and mission for each of us, and when we fulfill it, He makes His approval of us known. Remember at Jesus's baptism when God's voice came out of the heavens and said, "This is My beloved Son, in whom I am well pleased"? A dove descended and lit on the head of Jesus. We see God's glory descending as a sign of approval of the work of His Son. In our marketplace we can bring glory to God in whatever we do if we maintain a godly attitude and behave with actions that are pleasing to Him.

3. *Praise*

Praise is an expression of our gratitude toward God. Thanksgiving takes place when we breathe a prayer of thanks to God for His goodness. Praise results when we tell others about it. In the Hebrew vocabulary, there is no such word as "thanks." In our culture we grow up saying, "Thank you." That is our way of vocalizing our appreciation for kindnesses. It also is an expression of politeness in our society. But in the Old Testament there was no such word. Instead we find the term of praise, which means to let others know of the goodness or grace of God. We honor both God and the worker when we praise the person by saying, "You've sure made good use of the gifts and talents God has given you. Congratulations to you and praise be to God." This is a vital part of the glory of God. On the job, our lives should be expressions to others of the goodness of God.

4. *Priorities*

Our Lord gave us the greatest commandment: "You shall love the Lord your God with all your heart, and with all your soul, and with all your mind." The first commandment was, "You shall have no other gods before Me." Matthew 6 says, "Seek first [God's] kingdom and His righteousness; and all these things shall be added to you." God first. Nothing else equal. Unless God is made top priority in our lives we cannot know success at work or anywhere else. We begin to glorify God when people sense the supremacy of God in our lives.

Now, to apply these four words to our daily work situation, we can ask four questions. We can focus on the *prominence of God* by asking, "How can I have an awareness of God on the job?" We can concentrate on the *purpose of God* by asking the questions, "How can I fulfill the desires of God for my life on the job?" We can fix our attention on the *praise of God* by asking, "How can I be a constant expression of the praise of God on the job?" We can think seriously about the *priority of God* by asking, "How can I keep God first in my job?" Whatever you do, do it all for the glory of God.

Why are we to glorify Him? What happens when we glorify God at church each Sunday and lift up His name in praise on the job, in the home, even in the neighborhood? What happens when we regularly glorify God? Several things.

When we begin to glorify God, the smallest, minute, insignificant things begin to have meaning and purpose. That's why Paul said that when we glorify God even something as routine as eating

and drinking begins to have purpose. Our behavior becomes important. The mundane becomes meaningful. We begin to realize who
we are in God and what we can accomplish in Him. Glorifying
God is a faith-lifting experience. We think more highly of God,
of our brothers and sisters, and of our job. Redemptive lift is a
phrase that is used among Christian circles. It means that when
a person first comes in contact with God and establishes a personal
relationship with Jesus Christ, that person's whole life begins to
elevate. He becomes a more balanced person emotionally,
psychologically and mentally. He begins to develop right relationships with God and with his fellow man. He begins to think better
of himself and of others.

When I pastored in Lancaster, Ohio, our congregation ministered
to a reform school for boys eighteen and younger who had experienced problems with the law. We shared Christ with those boys.
One day the superintendent called me and said, "Pastor, we have
watched the boys you are working with and we have seen a drastic
change in their behavior in this institution." I told the superintendent
that I was pleased, but not surprised.

Paul said it, didn't he? "Therefore if any man is in Christ, he
is a new creature; the old things passed away; behold new things
have come." That is the redemptive lift. When you or anyone else
begins to glorify God, there is an elevation of yourself, your
surroundings, your situations. Have you ever, when you found
yourself in a desperate situation, begun to glorify God and lift
Him up? Suddenly your problems don't seem to be as difficult.
It always happens that way when we seek Him.

When Paul says we are to bring glory to God in our jobs. He
is saying that when we glorify God, our jobs begin to take on
new meaning and purpose.

It also moves us from fear to faith. When God's glory came
to the shepherds in Bethlehem, it moved them from fear to faith.
The disciples at Pentecost went from fear to faith. Paul, when he
was shipwrecked with other prisoners, was always confident that
the Lord stood by him. When we glorify God we always experience
the transition from fear to faith.

Additionally, when we glorify God, we make Him evident in
the small things as well as the large things. Too often we see God
just in the great things, like on Sunday morning at worship services
when there are hundreds of believers together. But we miss Him
at lunch break on Tuesday. When we can reverse that imbalance

and see Him the other six days a week as well, we then are glorifying God consistently.

And finally, we are to glorify God to keep our motives pure. This is something we have to wrestle with constantly, especially while on the job. Paul teaches us that principle in 1 Corinthians 10. Pure motives lead to solid testimonies.

APPLYING THE PRINCIPLES

Once we become convinced that our Christian walk should be as obvious at work as it is elsewhere, we become eager to be bold testimonies for Christ while we're on the job. However, this is easier said than done.

When we are at work we are mindful of the fact that people with authority have placed restrictions upon us. Our quotas, work shifts, break times, job descriptions and territories are often decided by other people. With such limitations put upon us, we may wonder if there will be adequate "elbow room" to exercise our Christian life.

Well, there can be. But it takes a plan. Let me explain.

The first thing you need to do is get a new job. Maybe you are thinking ironically, *Well, praise the Lord! I now have permission to change jobs. It was hard enough finding this one!* But I'm not talking about going to a different business place or changing occupations. You can, if you change your attitude, have a new job at your old job. The old employer can become a new employer. The old secretary can become a new secretary.

People and situations can become different for you, if you change your mind-set and attitude. Begin to look at them in a different light. When people come to me and are unhappy with their jobs, I don't try to change their employment. Instead, I try to change their attitude. I don't tell them to *look out* for new locations, I tell them to change their *outlook* at the present location.

What about you? Are you a job-jumper? Where are you looking for joy in your life? Where are you looking for meaning in life? If your only purpose is a paycheck, then you're in trouble. If your purpose for your job is just to squeeze out a living, that's a real problem. You need to change your attitude. Doing so will be like getting a whole new job.

At the first of each year people make New Year's resolutions. Most last only a few days. When you resolve to be a more effective witness on the job, you must be dedicated to your commitment.

Before you change any outward situation, begin to look inwardly —
at your heart, your motives, your mind and your attitude. Ask
yourself, "Why am I doing what I am doing?" God then will
begin to do a real work in your life.

Once there was a druggist who owned a store on the outskirts
of a small town. Often when newcomers would approach the town,
they would stop first at this drugstore. Many times they would
ask the druggist, "Is this a good town in which to live?"

The druggist would stand behind the counter, smile and reply,
"Let me ask you a question. How was the town you just left?"

Some people would say, "Well, one of the reasons we are
moving is because it wasn't a friendly town. People didn't help
you out and they really didn't care for their neighbors. You hardly
knew anybody."

The pharmacist would listen to them, smile, and say, "This
town's the same way. People aren't very friendly. They don't meet
your needs. You'll have a hard time getting along with them."

At other times someone else would come into the same store
and ask, "How is this town?"

And the druggist would answer, "How was the town you just
left?"

"Oh, it was a wonderful, warm town. People were kind, beautiful,
friendly to me."

The druggist then would reply, "That's the way this town is, too."

Isn't it amazing? Two people in the very same situation and
one can hardly wait to get out of it and the other can hardly wait
to get into it. One gets in the car on Monday morning, all excited
about work, and about what's going to happen. The other groans
all the way to the garage before he even gets into the car. You
get a new job by getting a new attitude.

*The second thing I would encourage you to do is go work for
a new boss.* You're thinking, "That's the answer — I need a new
boss!" Everyone works for somebody. No one is boss-free. The
guy out in the plant has a supervisor who walks around. That man
has a division head. And there's a director over the division head.
And the president is over the supervisors in the company. The
president, however, must report to the board of directors, who, in
turn, must report to the stockholders. Everyone has a boss.

When I write that you should get a new boss, I want you to
understand that your whole life is to glorify God. When you let
Him be the boss of your life and you are accountable to Him and

your meaning in life is to live for Him, then you will have a greater purpose. That doesn't mean that you ignore the boss on the organizational chart. In fact, Ephesians 6 tells us that the employer is to care for his employees and that the employees are to be honest and have integrity.

We are to serve our employers, not with eye service so that we work when they watch us, but instead we are to work with constant diligence so that we glorify God in everything we do. An employer has the same responsibility: to consider each person who works for him or her as a gift from God, and to know that helping that person achieve success is one of the major missions of a good employer. An employer's responsibility as an overseer of others is to come alongside people, to clarify their goals, to set up accountability systems and to help workers have a sense of worth in the midst of their work.

Third, I would encourage you to stop working for a living. I'm not proposing that you become lazy or irresponsible. But what I am reminding you of again is that when work is strictly for a paycheck, our lives become meaningless. The apostle Paul didn't say, "For to me, to live is to be a tentmaker." True, that's what he was. But he said, "For to me, to live is *Christ."* He could keep on making tents with a joyful heart and do so for the glory of God because he wasn't working for a living. He was living for his work for Jesus. It just so happened that to put bread on the table he made tents.

I recently had breakfast with one of my friends and we talked about this very thing. He has a wonderful job and there is no problem with it. But he said, "Pastor, what I'm trying to figure out is how I can serve God even better at my job and bring my colleagues into the knowledge and saving grace of the Lord Jesus." We had a one hour brainstorming session on how he could modify his job and make it a testimony to God. Soon, this man wasn't working just to make a living.

The fourth and last thing I would tell you to do is find a new company. No, not a new organization, but a new "company" of believers. Find someone to meet with on a regular basis. Find someone who will encourage you and walk with you in those tough times. You can minister and pray with one another. I know we become weary in well-doing but we need to surround ourselves with those who will lift us up and encourage us through that process. That which is closest to us begins to affect our entire attitude of life. You need to be around Christians who will hold you accountable and exhort and encourage and lift you up. If you don't, your negative surroundings will begin to discolor your whole life.

I love the story of the grandpa who went to see his grandchildren. He laid down one afternoon for a nap. He had a moustache and one of the grandsons could not resist temptation. He took some Limburger cheese and put it in grandpa's moustache. When grandpa woke up he began to sniff. He said, "This bedroom stinks." He got up off the bed and went to the kitchen where grandma was making some cookies. He sat down at the kitchen table and said, "Well, the kitchen stinks." He thought he would go outside and get a breath of fresh air. He went outside to the back yard and took a deep breath and said, "The whole world stinks!" Because grandpa had Limburger cheese in his moustache.

Do you have Limburger cheese in your mental moustache or do you perhaps surround yourself with people who constantly eat Limburger cheese? If so, your whole world is going to smell. I know there are people who go to work every Monday with Limburger cheese in their lunch bucket. Their ride to work stinks. And there is a Limburger cheese smell all around them and they can't get away from it.

The good news is, you can empty the lunch bucket and put the sweetness of the presence of God into it. He can give you a new attitude and you can be "on the job" for Him.